OSPREY AIRCRAFT OF THE ACES • 109

American Aces Against the Kamikaze

SERIES EDITOR: TONY HOLMES

OSPREY AIRCRAFT OF THE ACES • 109

American Aces Against the Kamikaze

Edward M Young

OSPREY
PUBLISHING

Front Cover

On the morning of 17 April 1945 a flight of six F4U-1D Corsairs of VF-84, flying off USS *Bunker Hill* **(CV-17), launched on a combat air patrol (CAP) to cover a destroyer on radar picket duty some 75 miles northeast of Okinawa. Lt Doris 'Chico' Freeman, who had completed a previous combat tour with VF-17 in the Solomons in 1943-44, where he had claimed two 'Zekes', was leading one of the divisions. Earlier that morning the Imperial Japanese Navy's Fifth Air Fleet had despatched a force of 30 kamikaze with an escort of 62 A6M-5 Zero-sen and 34 N1K2-J Shiden-Kai ('George') fighters, possibly from the 601st Kokutai. The latter machines were assigned the task of keeping the route of advance and withdrawal clear of American fighters.**

Soon after arriving on station the VF-84 flight spotted a lone 'George' fighter ten miles west of the destroyer, this aircraft having most likely separated from the main flight. Seeing the Corsairs, the Japanese pilot dropped his fuel tank and attempted to escape. Opening the throttle on his Corsair, Lt Doris 'Chico' Freeman easily gained on the 'George', despite choosing not to jettison his belly tank. Pulling in behind the Japanese fighter, Freeman opened fire from the 'six o'clock level' position and saw his rounds have an immediate effect on the enemy aircraft, hitting the left wing root and, in all likelihood, killing the pilot. The 'George' fell away to the left and crashed into the sea. This was Lt Freeman's second of six kills during the Okinawa campaign. He would go on to claim two Ki-97 'Nates' on 28 April and two more Nakajima fighters on 11 May, giving him a total of nine victories in two combat tours.

Freeman was killed just hours after his final victories when two kamikaze aircraft crashed into *Bunker Hill* **and destroyed VF-84's ready room (***Cover artwork by Mark Postlethwaite***)**

First published in Great Britain in 2012 by Osprey Publishing
Midland House, West Way, Botley, Oxford, OX2 0PH
44-02 23rd Street, Suite 219, Long Island City, NY, 11101, USA

E-mail; info@ospreypublishing.com

Osprey Publishing is part of the Osprey Group

A CIP catalogue record for this book is available from the British Library

ISBN: 978 1 84908 745 2
PDF e-book ISBN: 978 1 84908 746 9
e-Pub ISBN: 978 1 78200 289 5

Edited by Tony Holmes
Page design by Tony Truscott
Cover Artwork by Mark Postlethwaite
Aircraft Profiles by Mark Styling
Index by Alan Thatcher
Originated by PDQ Digital Media Solutions
Printed and bound in China through Bookbuilders

12 13 14 15 16 17   10 9 8 7 6 5 4 3 2 1

Osprey Publishing is supporting the Woodland Trust, the UK's leading woodland conservation charity, by funding the dedication of trees.

www.ospreypublishing.com

ACKNOWLEDGEMENTS

I would like to acknowledge several people who assisted me in the preparation of this volume. I owe a debt of gratitude to Frank Olynyk for the tremendous amount of research he has done over many years compiling lists of USAAF, US Navy and Marine Corps aerial claims in World War 2. His victory lists for the Pacific War were invaluable during the creation of this book. Sarah Serizawa patiently translated the Japanese material on JAAF and IJN Special Attack units, despite a demanding academic schedule. In 2010 Phil Schasker kindly arranged for me to attend a reunion of VF-17 aces, where Willis Hardy, Charles Watts, the late James Pearce and Tillman Pool graciously consented to interviews. Phil was also generous in sharing recordings of World War 2 Fighter Aces Symposiums that the Northern California Friends of the American Fighter Aces Association had presented in the past. Col Dean Caswell USMC (Ret) gave me permission to quote from his memoir of VMF-221, *Fighting Falcons – The Saga of Marine Fighter Squadron VMF-221.* Jack Lambert provided a number of photos of 318th FG aeroplanes, while Amy Heidrick at the Museum of Flight responded wonderfully to a last minute request for photographs from his collection. Finally, Holly Reed and her staff at the Still Pictures Reference, National Archives and Records Service, provided excellent and patient support during several visits. To all, my sincere thanks.

CONTENTS

THE BEGINNING

At 0729 hrs on the morning of 25 October 1944, radar on the escort carriers of Task Force 77.4.1 (call sign 'Taffy 1'), cruising off the Philippine island of Mindanao, picked up Japanese aeroplanes approaching through the scattered cumulous clouds. The carriers immediately went to General Quarters on what had already been an eventful morning. Using the clouds as cover, the Japanese aircraft managed to reach a point above 'Taffy 1' without being seen. Suddenly, at 0740 hrs, an A6M5 Reisen dived out of the clouds directly into the escort carrier USS *Santee* (CVE-29), crashing through its flightdeck on the port side forward of the elevator.

Just 30 seconds later a second 'Zeke' dived towards the USS *Suwannee* (CVE-27), while a third targeted USS *Petrof Bay* (CVE-80) – anti-aircraft artillery (AAA) fire managed to shoot down both fighters. Then, at 0804 hrs, a fourth 'Zeke' dived on the *Petrof Bay*, but when hit by AAA it swerved and crashed into the flightdeck of *Suwanee*, blowing a hole in it forward of the aft elevator. Aboard *Santee* and *Suwannee* 62 men had been killed and 82 wounded in little more than 20 minutes.

Three hours later it was 'Taffy 3's' turn to experience this new menace. Having just narrowly escaped annihilation at the hands of the battleships of the Imperial Japanese Navy's Central Force with the loss of only one vessel (USS *Gambier Bay* (CVE-73)), the escort carriers of 'Taffy 3' came under attack shortly before 1100 hrs. Five 'Zeke' fighters approached at low altitude, then pulled up sharply to around 5000 ft and commenced

Magazines on USS *St Lo* (CVE-63) explode after the first ever kamikaze attack on 25 October 1944. *St Lo* sank within 30 minutes of being hit (National Museum of Naval Aviation (NMNA))

their dives onto their targets. USS *Kitkun Bay* (CVE-71) was the first to be hit when a 'Zeke' dived directly at the ship's bridge, passed over the island, hit the port catwalk and crashed into the sea alongside the vessel. Two more 'Zekes' then targeted USS *White Plains* (CVE-66), pulling out of their dives when faced with a wall of AAA. One came back to attack *White Plains* again, crashing just alongside.

At 1052 hrs the second 'Zeke', on fire from AAA hits, dove on USS *St Lo* (CVE-63) and crashed through its flightdeck into the hangar deck below, setting off the vessel's magazines in a huge explosion. Fatally damaged, *St Lo* sank 29 minutes later at the cost of 114 lives. Three 'Zekes' then attacked USS *Kalinin Bay* (CVE-68), one hitting the flightdeck before crashing overboard, the second striking the port stack and catwalk and the third missing the carrier to the port side.

The sailors and airmen of Task Force (TF) 77.4's escort carriers had been witnesses to Japan's new weapon of desperation – the first organised employment of pilots to deliberately crash their aircraft into American warships at the sacrifice of their lives. That morning the attacking Japanese aviators dove into their targets with no chance, or intention, of escape in an act that was incomprehensible to most Americans. To them, it was simple suicide, and the actions of the Japanese pilots were deemed to be suicide attacks – a term that came to be used to describe any attempt to crash into an Allied naval ship. Shortly after these initial attacks a new term would enter the American military vocabulary – kamikaze.

ORIGIN OF THE KAMIKAZE

'If only we might fall,
Like cherry blossoms in the Spring,
So pure and radiant!'

This was the haiku of a kamikaze pilot killed in February 1945 that was quoted in Ivan Morris' *The Nobility of Failure*.

The kamikaze emerged from Japan's increasingly desperate military predicament, the failure of its conventional forces and long-standing Japanese cultural traditions. The loss of Saipan and the defeat of the Imperial Japanese Navy (IJN) in June 1944 was a devastating blow that brought a reconsideration of Japan's future strategy. It was clear that the Americans would continue their inexorable advance across the Pacific, and it seemed that there was little the Japanese military could do to stop them. Japan's connections to its Southeast Asian sources of fuel and vital raw materials for its war industries were now directly threatened.

Having cast the conflict as a battle of annihilation between Japan and the Western countries – a battle 'to determine who shall devour and who shall be devoured' – the Japanese military saw no alternative but to continue the war. It was hoped that some way could be found to force the US military into a decisive battle that would inflict punishing losses on American forces leading to a Japanese victory. With both the army and navy expecting the next American operation to be an invasion of the Philippines, the Imperial General Headquarters in Japan agreed to commit the maximum number of troops, ships and aircraft possible in order to obtain certain victory.

There were, however, growing doubts in the minds of some senior officers about the ability of Japan's conventional forces to overcome American quantitative and qualitative superiority. The Battle of the Philippine Sea in June 1944 had conclusively demonstrated the IJN's inferiority to the US Navy. The IJN had little hope of replacing its lost aircraft carriers in time, much less building up a larger carrier fleet, and only a few of the newer carrier- and land-based aircraft beginning to enter service could match their American counterparts on equal terms. The Japanese Army Air Force (JAAF) was in little better shape, as it too possessed few aircraft that could challenge their US opponents.

Neither service could count on a substantial increase in new aircraft either. Japanese wartime aircraft production peaked in September 1944 and then began a terminal decline. Worse was the lack of experienced combat pilots. Relentless attrition over the Solomon Islands, New Guinea, Burma and China, and the carrier battles in the Central Pacific had robbed the JAAF and IJN of their best pilots and leaders. While both services had greatly expanded pilot training during 1943-44, the quality of pilots entering combat units had steadily declined. The combination of technically inferior aircraft and poorly trained pilots was reflected in ever higher rates of attrition. By the middle of 1944 the IJN was regularly experiencing loss rates of 60 per cent or greater in attacks on American forces, with little result.

It is little wonder that senior officers in both the IJN and JAAF, in their desperation, began to look for radical alternatives to conventional weapons, especially for attacks on US Navy aircraft carriers, which were the vanguards of American invasion forces. There had been several instances during the war of pilots using Tai-atari ('body-crashing') tactics against the enemy, deliberately ramming their aeroplanes into an American ship or aircraft. As the course of the war turned against Japan, several senior JAAF and IJN officers recommended jibaku (suicide) attacks as a means of overcoming American quantitative superiority, but up until the fall of Saipan the high command had refused to countenance such tactics as an official policy. Following the defeat at Saipan attitudes began to change.

That August the IJN approved, quietly and in great secrecy, production of a rocket-powered, piloted, flying bomb to be launched from a mother aeroplane for attacks against American warships. Built at the IJN's arsenal at Yokosuka as the MXY7 Ohka (Cherry Blossom), this new weapon was intentionally designed for pilots with limited flight training who would be making a one-way mission, guiding their aircraft into the enemy vessel at the sacrifice of their own life. In October 1944 the Kaigun Jinrai Butai (Navy Thunder Gods Corps) was set up to operate the new weapon under the designation of the 721st Kokutai. Once the piloted, rocket-assisted, glide bomb programme had been approved, it was not a great mental leap to take the next logical step – conversion of conventional aircraft into body-crashing suicide weapons for kesshi ('dare to die') attacks.

The concept of deliberate suicide was alien to American culture, but had a long historical tradition within Japan among Samurai warriors. When faced with failure or defeat, a warrior could commit ritual suicide to preserve his honour. Linked to this tradition was another – the warrior who sacrifices himself for a cause that he knows is hopeless, but does so out of sincerity and a sense of duty, as well as honour. This tradition – what the scholar Ivan Morris termed 'the nobility of failure' – has a deep resonance within Japanese culture. Throughout Japan's long history there have been unique individuals who supported a lost cause, believing it to be a just cause, and at the end chose suicide in the face of defeat. They became some of Japan's most noted heroes. The young JAAF and IJN pilots who chose to sacrifice themselves in suicide attacks fall into this tradition.

In his book *Thunder Gods - The Kamikaze Pilots Tell Their Story*, Hatsuho Naito explains the three strands in Japanese culture – Shintoism, Buddhism and Confucianism – that contributed to the Samurai ethos and provided a motivation for many suicide pilots. In the Shinto belief system, a warrior who died a heroic death would become both a 'warrior god' and one of the guardian spirits of the nation. Buddhism taught the impermanence of all things and the transitory nature of all life, exemplified in Japan through the fragile beauty of the cherry blossom. The Chinese Confucian tradition emphasised loyalty to the emperor, to superiors and to family. Duty and loyalty, even at the cost of one's own life, became linked through tradition and historical examples. The Imperial Rescript to Soldiers and Sailors, issued in 1882, made the linkage explicit.

In pledging loyalty to the Emperor of Japan, who embodied the nation, soldiers and sailors were told 'with a single heart fulfil your essential duty of loyalty and bear in mind that duty is weightier than a mountain, while death is lighter than a feather'. A further cultural concept, that of Giri ('obligation', or the 'burden of obligation'), was another strong motivation for many young pilots who felt a powerful sense of obligation to their parents and families and chose self-sacrifice in battle as a means of fulfilling this obligation. When calls went out for volunteers for what were deliberate suicide missions, with no chance of escape, the pilots and airmen who had to make the choice carried with them the weight of all these traditions, as well as the knowledge of Japan's desperate plight.

In early October 1944, Vice-Adm Takijiro Onishi, soon to be appointed commander of the Dai 1 Koku Kantai (1st Air Fleet) in the Philippines, requested approval from the Chief of the Naval General Staff to form a Special Attack unit to carry out body-crashing attacks against American warships. Initially opposed to the idea of suicide attacks, Onishi had come to accept that conventional attacks had little chance of success against the overwhelming power of the US Navy's Pacific Fleet. Like many Japanese military men, Onishi believed that his country's presumed spiritual and moral superiority could overcome America's material strength. A demonstration of Japan's spiritual power through suicide attacks would, many believed, thoroughly demoralise American military forces, as well as inflicting punishing losses. Onishi arrived in Manila on 17 October 1944 – the day preliminary operations for the American invasion of Leyte began – determined to carry out his plans.

On his arrival Onishi found that the Dai 1 Koku Kantai had little more than 40 operational aeroplanes. With invasion imminent, Imperial General Headquarters in Tokyo initiated Operation *Sho-Go 1* for the

Vice-Adm Takijiro Onishi, considered the father of the kamikaze, the IJN's Special Attack Corps (Naval History and Heritage Command (NHHC) NH-73093)

defence of the Philippines. Plans called for surface forces of the IJN to annihilate the invasion fleet in Leyte Gulf. On 19 October Onishi met with the senior officers of the 201st Kokutai at Mabalacat airfield, north of Manila, and issued a remarkable request.

The mission of the 1st Air Fleet was to provide air cover for the surface forces attacking Leyte Gulf. Onishi was convinced that the only way to successfully achieve this was to arm Zero-sen fighters with 250-kg bombs and use them in body-crashing attacks on the American carriers. He wanted the 201st Kokutai to organise a Special Attack unit, or Shimpu (Kamikaze) Tokubetsu Kogekitai (Divine Wind Special Attack unit), composed entirely of volunteers. Onishi had chosen the name of the unit deliberately. Kamikaze is an alternate, vernacular reading of the Chinese ideographs for Shimpu, or 'Divine Wind' – a reference to the famous storm that destroyed the Mongol invasion fleet off the coast of Japan in 1281. Onishi was asking his pilots to become like a Divine Wind to shatter the American invasion fleet.

Lt Yuko Seki, a carrier bomber pilot, agreed to command the first Special Attack unit, composed of 26 Zero-sen fighters divided into four units, each bearing a name resonant with history and cultural meaning taken from a famous Japanese poem – Yamato (the ancient name for Japan), Shikishima (the poetic name for Yamato), Asahi (the rising sun, a symbol of Japan) and Yamazakura (the mountain cherry blossom). Two of these units, Shikishima, flying from Mabalacat, and Yamato, flying from the island of Cebu, carried out the Special Attack unit's first successful suicide missions on 25 October 1944. The Yamato unit, flying from Cebu, attacked TF 77.4.1 ('Taffy 1'). Shortly thereafter, the Shikishima unit attacked TF 77.4.3 ('Taffy 3'). The results of these attacks appeared to be a vindication of Vice-Adm Onishi's forceful

Vice-Adm Onishi with one of the first groups of Special Attack pilots in the Philippines in late October 1944 (US Naval Institute 10150688)

advocacy of special attacks – one American carrier was sunk and four more seemingly severely damaged.

The Japanese people soon learned of the Special Attack units' efforts in the Philippines. IJN communiques lauded the 'sure hit, sure death, heroes of the sky', describing the Kamikaze Force as 'a special attack force of patriotic self-abandonment which takes upon itself the functions of a bomb, and whose members unite perfectly in one explosive charge the quality of a human bullet and the science of

Groundcrew and fellow pilots wave as a Special Attack pilot taxis his A6M5 Reisen ('Zeke') out for takeoff from a base in the Philippines in October-November 1944 (Robert Lawson Collection, NMNA)

destroying enemy ships'. Praising the Special Attack unit as 'the essence of the spirit of Bushido', a communique issued on 8 November 1944 went on to say 'how sublime is the form of the young flyer who, like clear undisturbed water, moves along winning our envy, and endeavours to live, with a smile, for a perpetually great cause'.

From early November 1944, these communiques began referring to the 'Kamikaze Special Attack Corps' and 'sure-death and sure-hit' attacks, often listing the Special Attack units by name, and explaining that they were composed of Japanese pilots who crashed their aeroplanes directly into their targets.

OPERATIONS IN THE PHILIPPINES

The apparent success of the kamikaze attacks of 25 October and the failure of conventional forces to defeat the US Navy in the Battle of Leyte Gulf brought more converts to the use of special attack tactics. The next day Vice-Adm Shigeru Fukutome, commander of the Dai 2 Koku Kantai (2nd Air Fleet), which had moved to the Philippines from Formosa on 23 October, agreed to the formation of a second Special Attack Corps. The 701st Kokutai, a land-based bomber air group, quickly formed the Second Shimpu (Kamikaze) Tokubetsu Kogekitai (Second Divine Wind Special Attack unit, later shortened to Shinbutai, meaning 'special' – a euphemism for kamikaze units) with four kamikaze units, namely Chuyu ('Fidelity and Courage'), Seichu ('True Loyalty and Patriotism'), Juncho ('True Faith') and Giretsu ('Gallantry and Chivalry').

While the First Divine Wind Special Attack unit continued to use A6M5 Zero-sen fighters, the 701st Kokutai's Second Shimpu (Kamikaze) Tokubetsu Kogekitai employed the Yokosuka D4Y Suisei Carrier Bomber ('Judy') and the older Aichi D3A Type 99 Carrier Bomber ('Val').

The Second Shimpu (Kamikaze) Tokubetsu Kogekitai flew its first kamikaze mission on the afternoon of 27 October 1944, when the Shuyu, Giretsu and Junchu units sent off three and two Suisei and a single 'Val', respectively, from Nichols Field, near Manila, to attack shipping in Leyte Gulf. The 1st and 2nd Air Fleets had by now been combined into the Number 1 Combined Land-Based Flying Fleet under Vice-Adm Fukutome, with Vice-Adm Onishi as his Chief-of-Staff.

Special Attack units now became an integral part of operations against American forces. There was no shortage of volunteers.

The Special Attack units soon developed standard tactics for kamikaze attacks. Aeroplanes would go out in small numbers, typically two to six in number, with another two to six Zero-sen fighters as escorts to ward off American fighters and to report the results of the kamikaze attacks. The IJN's Special Attack units believed that smaller formations had a better chance of sneaking up on American formations. During the Philippine campaign attacks with ten or more kamikaze took place on relatively few occasions.

The approach to the target was done from high altitude (18,000-21,000 ft), with a gradually steepening dive onto the target, or from very low altitude to avoid American radar, the kamikaze pilot popping up to 1200-1500 ft and then diving steeply into the ship. As the original kamikaze units disappeared in combat, new ones were hurriedly formed to replace them. The Third Shimpu Tokubetsu Kogekitai was formed at the end of October, the Fourth Shimpu Tokubetsu Kogekitai in early November and the Fifth Shimpu Tokubetsu Kogekitai later that same month. The 201st Kokutai contributed pilots, Zero-sen fighters and some Suisei carrier bombers for the new Special Attack units until the end of the campaign. More volunteers came from the air groups that were hurriedly being thrown into combat in the Philippines. The 203rd, 221st, 341st and 653rd Kokutai brought more Zero-sens, while the 763rd Kokutai provided volunteers flying the Yokosuka P1Y Ginga ('Frances'). Towards the very end of the campaign volunteers from the 765th Kokutai brought their Suisei to the Special Attack units.

Smaller kamikaze flights were organised within the larger Special Attack units, often taking symbolic cultural or patriotic names such as Umehana (plum blossom), Shirotora (White Tiger), Sakura (cherry blossom) and Shikajima (Deer Island). In the desperate last weeks of the Philippine battle these smaller flights were often simply labelled Kingotai (flight) – one of the last kamikaze attacks in the first week of January 1945 was flown by the 30th Kingotai.

Not to be outdone, the JAAF sent its own Special Attack units to the Philippines. After the fall of Saipan the Army had also begun to plan for

Pilots and crewmen from the JAAF's Kyokko-Tai Special Attack Unit receive a farewell toast before heading off on a kamikaze mission. This unit flew Type 99 Light Bombers ('Lily') (Author's collection)

A Type 99 Assault Aeroplane ('Sonia') from the Army Sekicho-tai Special Attack unit takes off from Bacalod, on the island of Negros, for a kamikaze mission during December 1944 (Author's collection)

body-crashing attacks against American warships The first two Army Shinbutai units – the Banda-tai, equipped with the Kawasaki Type 99 Twin-engined Light Bomber ('Lily'), and the Fugaku-tai, flying the Mitsubishi Type 4 Heavy Bomber ('Peggy') – had been organised in Japan in the late summer of 1944 and arrived in the Philippines at the end of October.

The Banda-tai set off on its first kamikaze sortie on 5 November 1944, but it ran into US Navy carrier fighters over its base at Nichols Field and lost several aircraft. A week later the unit sent out three 'Lily' bombers to Leyte Gulf, Japan's Domei news agency claiming the destruction of one battleship and a transport by the Banda-tai. The Fugaku-tai began Shinbutai attacks the next day.

In early November the 4th Kokugun (4th Air Army), charged with the defence of the Philippines, was given permission to organise its own Special Attack units, drawing volunteers from the tactical fighter and fighter-bomber squadrons under its command. Most of the JAAF Special Attack units organised in the Philippines employed the Army Type 1 Fighter Hayabusa ('Oscar') and the Army Type 99 Assault Aeroplane ('Sonia'), carrying various sizes of bombs. Like their IJN counterparts, the JAAF Shinbutai units sent out small numbers of kamikaze (sometimes only a single aircraft).

In planning for a possible invasion of the Philippines, the Japanese Imperial General Headquarters decided to commit as much of Japan's air and ground forces as possible to ensure a decisive victory over the enemy. Once the invasion began more air units were rushed to the battle zone and thrown into combat. Imperial General Headquarters had decided that the JAAF should concentrate its attacks on the American invasion fleet, particularly the troop transports, while IJN air units would attack the aircraft carriers supporting the invasion. This was not a strict division, and in practice both JAAF and IJN aeroplanes launched attacks on both groups of targets.

Once Special Attack tactics had been adopted, the kamikaze missions were flown in conjunction with conventional attacks. Kamikaze strikes on American ships continued until early January 1945 when, with the American invasion of Luzon, the airfields in the central part of the Philippine island that served as bases for both JAAF and IJN Special Attack units became untenable. By then the latter had run out of pilots and aeroplanes.

THE AMERICAN RESPONSE

American strategic planning for the re-conquest of the Philippines envisioned the capture of one of the nation's southern islands for use as a base for an advance north to Luzon. The final plan adopted in the autumn of 1944 called for the invasion of Leyte on 20 October and the invasion of Mindoro on 5 December to provide airfields to support the invasion of Luzon, planned for 20 December 1944.

The US Navy's carrier forces would be heavily involved providing air support for these invasions. Gen Douglas MacArthur, Supreme Commander, Allied Forces Southwest Pacific, requested that Adm William Halsey's Third Fleet, with the Fast Carrier Task Force 38, provide air support for the invasion until Gen Kenny's Fifth Air Force fighter groups could move up to Leyte and take over. The air plan called for TF 38 to hand over to the Fifth Air Force a week after the initial landings on Leyte. TF 38 had nine *Essex*-class fleet carriers and eight *Independence*-class light carriers assigned to four Task Groups (TG 38.1, TG 38.2, TG 38.3 and TG 38.4), with 561 F6F Hellcat fighters in addition to 497 TBM Avenger and SB2C Helldiver torpedo- and dive-bombers. Supplementing the Fast Carrier Task Force, the Seventh Fleet's Escort Carrier Group TF 77.4 had 18 escort carriers to provide close air support and protection for the invasion fleet, with 61 F6F Hellcats, 243 FM-2 Wildcats and 210 TBM Avengers.

Weather soon forced the air plan to go awry. Heavy rains in the weeks following the invasion turned the airfields on Leyte into mud, resulting in airfield construction falling far behind schedule. Fifth Air Force fighter squadrons dribbled in as soon as they could be accommodated, but it was not until late November that the Fifth Air Force assumed responsibility for air operations over Leyte. As a result, TF 38 had to provide air support well beyond the planned handover date. The JAAF and IJN had responded to the Leyte invasion with heavy conventional and kamikaze attacks against the ships lying offshore and on the airfield at Tacloban. JAAF fighters and bombers alone flew more than 1000 sorties over Leyte. Kamikaze attacks, though fewer in number, greatly increased the risk to American invasion fleets and complicated their defence. During the month of November the kamikaze sank or damaged nearly 40 warships and transports.

Beginning on 28 October, and continuing until 25 November, the Fast Carriers attacked targets in the Viyasan Islands (Cebu, Leyte, Negros, Paney and Samar) and made repeated strikes on the airfields on Luzon to disrupt the JAAF's and IJN's ability to launch conventional and kamikaze attacks against Leyte. The Fast Carriers returned to hit the Luzon airfields in mid-December in support of the invasion of Mindoro. Since the Special Attack units were using the same types as the regular conventional fighter and bomber units, any aircraft shot down or destroyed on the ground was one less that could potentially be used in a kamikaze attack.

In the course of these strikes during October-December 1944 a number of pilots managed to shoot down five or more Japanese aeroplanes, including two pilots who became 'aces in a day'. High scorers during this period were Lt Cecil Harris of VF-18 and Lt Cdr Leonard Check of VF-7, both with nine victories, and VF-80's Lt Patrick Fleming with seven. Harris' victories during the final

Lt Cecil Harris of VF-18 (right) with Cdr David McCampbell, the US Navy's ranking ace of World War 2. Harris scored nine victories over the Philippines after the onset of the kamikaze attacks (NARA 80G-47684)

months of 1944 would bring his total to 23, making him the second-highest scoring US Navy ace at the time. Patrick Fleming would add additional kills in later battles to end the war as one of the US Navy's leading aces with 19 victories.

TF 38's air groups hit the Japanese airstrips around Clark Field for the first time on 29 October, claiming 80 Japanese aircraft shot down. Flying off the carrier USS *Intrepid* (CV-11), Lt Cecil Harris of VF-18 managed to shoot down three Army Type 2 Fighters ('Tojos') and a single 'Zeke'. Squadronmate Lt(jg) Robert Hurst claimed three 'Zekes' in the first strike to the Clark Field area, and then shot down another 'Zeke' and a 'Tojo' in the afternoon to become an 'ace in a day'.

Following heavy Japanese air attacks on Tacloban, the Fast Carriers launched another series of strikes on the Luzon airfields on 5-6 November, shooting down 97 aircraft on the 5th and 22 on the 6th, as well as destroying several hundred more on the ground. During the 5 November raid Lt Patrick Fleming scored his first victory, shooting down a 'Zeke' over Manila Bay. Another ace who claimed multiple kills that day was Lt Charles Stimpson of VF-11, who downed two 'Oscars' and a 'Tojo' over the Clark Field area.

The Fast Carriers returned to Luzon again on 13-14 November and their fighter pilots were credited with 19 victories. Naval aircraft made a final strike on the Luzon airfields in support of the Leyte invasion on 25 November, claiming 52 aircraft shot down. Lt Harris was among the victors on this date, downing three 'Tojos' and a 'Hamp' over Nielsen Field – the fourth occasion during which he had claimed three or more victories in a single day.

F6F-5 Hellcats from VF-80 on board USS *Ticonderoga* (CV-14) prepare for a mission over the Philippines in November 1944. Lt Patrick Fleming claimed seven Japanese aircraft flying with VF-80 during the Philippines campaign (NARA 80G-258610)

A 'Zeke' comes under the guns of a US Navy Hellcat during the October-November 1944 battles over the Philippines (NARA 80G-46984)

Delays in completing the capture of Leyte forced the postponement of the Mindoro invasion until 15 December 1944 and the Luzon invasion to 9 January 1945. In support of the Mindoro operation, TF 38 attacked the airfields north of Manila. From 14 to 16 December carrier aircraft made repeated strikes, destroying some 200 Japanese aeroplanes in the air and on the ground. Several pilots did well on 14 December, which was the most successful day in terms of Japanese aircraft destroyed. Over Clark Field in the early morning, Lt(jg) Douglas Baker of VF-20 downed three 'Zekes' and an 'Oscar'. These were his last victories of the war, and they took his tally of claims to 16.333.

Late in the afternoon Lt Patrick Fleming led off two divisions of VF-80 fighters from USS *Ticonderoga* (CV-14). Tasked with attacking the Luzon airfields, Fleming's divisions ran into a large formation of 'Zekes' and 'Oscars' southwest of Vigan, on the west coast of Luzon. Despite their numerical inferiority, the American pilots immediately attacked. In the combats that followed, Lt Robert Anderson managed to shoot down five 'Zekes' to become an 'ace in a day', while Lt Patrick Fleming claimed four. Their compatriot, Lt Richard Cormier, who would become an ace during the Tokyo strikes in February 1945, also claimed four victories for his first combat successes.

The large aircraft carriers of TF 38 were priority targets for the IJN's Special Attack units. Cruising off the coast of Luzon, the Fast Carriers came under kamikaze attacks on several occasions. *Intrepid*, USS *Franklin* (CV-13) and the light carrier USS *Belleau Wood* (CVL-24) were hit during the 29-30 October strikes on Luzon, USS *Lexington* (CV-16) on 5 November and, on 25 November, USS *Essex* (CV-9), *Intrepid* again, USS *Hancock* (CV-19) and USS *Cabot* (CVL-28).

While it is difficult to definitively link aerial victories over the kamikaze to a specific carrier fighter ace (a pilot shooting down a Japanese fighter might not know whether it was on a kamikaze or a conventional mission), there are at least two instances when it seems highly probable.

During the afternoon of 29 October, the Second Shimpu (Kamikaze) Tokubetsu Kogekitai sent out five 'Vals' from its Seichu-tai, Shimbu-tai and Shimpei-tai units, with an escort of Zero-sen fighters, to attack the Fast Carriers off the coast of Luzon. At 1615 hrs Lt Cdr Leonard Check, CO of VF-7 (which was embarked in *Hancock*), was flying a CAP over TG 38.2 when he was directed to intercept approaching enemy aircraft. Check saw a group of seven 'Vals' in a diamond formation at 17,000 ft, with eight escorting Zero-sen fighters above them. He shot down one 'Val' in an overhead run and then quickly downed another as the Japanese aircraft scattered.

Check then decided to go after the 'Vals', since they were the main threat to the Task Force. He fired at two dive-bombers flying in formation, without result. One of the 'Vals' did a split-S and Check went after him, firing, only to find that his guns had jammed because of the negative acceleration. The 'Val' repeated this tactic, but Check finally managed to clear his guns and get in an effective burst, sending the

An F6F-5 Hellcat from VF-7, commanded by Lt Cdr Leonard Check, commences its takeoff run along the flightdeck of USS *Hancock* (CV-19) at the start of a fighter sweep over Luzon in October 1944 (NARA 80G-285973)

dive-bomber into the ocean. Climbing back up to 3000 ft, he saw his fourth 'Val', which also went into a split-S. Check fired a burst that hit the 'Val's' cockpit, killing the pilot and sending the aeroplane crashing into the water. Shortly thereafter he shot at a 'Zeke' in a head-on pass, claiming it as a probable. For his actions that afternoon Check was awarded the Navy Cross.

On 25 November two units of the Fifth Shimpu (Kamikaze) Tokubetsu Kogekitai – the Toppu-tai and the Kyofu-tai – sent off four 'Frances' bombers from the 762nd and 763rd Kokutai, with several Zero-sen fighter escorts, between 1143 hrs and 1230 hrs as part of a large kamikaze attack on the Fast Carrier Force off Luzon. At around 1350 hrs Lt Patrick Fleming and his wingman, Ens Paul Beaudry, were flying a communications relay mission off the coast of Luzon when they spotted a formation of Japanese aeroplanes. Fleming and Beaudry immediately attacked, the former shooting down two 'Frances' and Beaudry a third.

Recalling the impact of the kamikaze attacks in a post-war interview, Adm James S 'Jimmy' Thach, then a commander serving as Operations Officer to Vice-Adm John McCain, commander of TG 38.1, said that the kamikaze 'was a weapon, for all practical purposes, far ahead of its time. It was actually a guided missile before we had any such thing as guided missiles. It was guided by a human brain, human eyes and hands, and even better than a guided missile, it could look, digest the information and change course, thus avoiding damage, and get to the target. So we had to do something about this'. The immediate need was for more fighter aircraft.

During December the fighter complement of the air groups on the larger *Essex*-class carriers was increased from 54 to 72, reducing the number of dive- and torpedo-bombers from 42 to 30. For ease of administration these extra-large fighter units were later split into one fighter (VF) and one fighter-bomber (VBF) squadron, each with 36 aircraft. TF 38 developed a dawn-to-dusk system of CAPs that covered low, medium and high altitudes. Thach came up with a system called the 'Big Blue Blanket' to provide nearly constant coverage of Japanese airfields when the Fast Carriers were in range of land-based aeroplanes.

Although they did not have the same opportunities as the fighter pilots on the fast carriers, the naval aviators flying FM-2 Wildcats with the Composite Squadrons serving aboard the escort carriers did engage in combat with conventional and kamikaze aircraft on a number of occasions while providing CAPs over the invasion fleets. VC-27, flying off USS *Savo Island* (CVE-78), was the most successful Composite Squadron during the Philippines campaign with 61.5 victories. The unit produced one ace, Lt Ralph Elliott (who was also the squadron commander), who claimed nine victories, and two 'near aces' in Ens Thomas Mackie and Robert Pfeifer, who shot down 4.5 aircraft each.

Lt Elliott had several possible encounters with kamikaze. In the late afternoon of 27 October 1944, he was leading his division on a CAP over the invasion fleet off Leyte when, at 1700 hrs, Elliott spotted a formation of seven 'Vals' at 10,000 ft. This may have been a group of kamikaze from the Junchu-tai and the Seichu-tai units of the Second Shimpu (Kamikaze) Tokubetsu Kogekitai that had set off from Nichols Field for Leyte at 1530 hrs. Elliott and his wingman chased one of the dive-bombers, getting in several bursts. The 'Val' spun out of control and crashed on Leyte.

Then, on 15 December, while on a CAP over the Mindoro invasion fleet, Elliott encountered a single 'Oscar', possibly from the JAAF's Ichi-U-tai unit (which sent out three Ki-43s on kamikaze missions that day), setting up for an attack on the ships below. Manoeuvring to escape the Wildcats, the 'Oscar' pilot turned into Elliott's FM-2. He got in several good bursts, getting on the tail of the JAAF fighter, where he fired again, setting the 'Oscar' on fire and then watching it crash into the sea below.

Lt Elliott and Ens Pfeifer were both involved in VC-27's most productive day, 5 January 1945, when the squadron shot down 15 aircraft while flying CAPs over some of the units of TF 77 that were sailing north to Lingayan Gulf for the invasion of Luzon. The kamikaze were out in force this day, IJN Special Attack units sending out around 30 kamikaze aeroplanes against the US fleet in one of the largest attacks of the Philippine campaign. The 201st Kokutai contributed 17 Zero-sen fighters to the 18th Kingotai for the attack, taking off at 1557 hrs from the airfield at Mabalacat.

Lt Elliott was leading a division of FM-2s on CAP at 17,000 ft, with a second division led by Lt Roger

VC-27 was the highest-scoring Composite Squadron during the Philippines campaign. The wheels of this VC-27 FM-2 Wildcat collapsed following a heavy landing aboard USS *Savo Island* (CVE-78) (NARA 80G-381794)

Mulcahy at 12,000 ft. At 1645 hrs many bogies were reported approaching the Task Force, and in the ensuing interceptions the two divisions became separated. Elliott and his wingman, Ens James Manfrin, were vectored out and found a Ki-61 'Tony' flying at 3000 ft. The two pilots made multiple passes on the Japanese aircraft, and its pilot used skillful manoeuvring to avoid getting hit for as long as possible. Finally, Elliott managed to get onto the 'Tony's' tail and send it crashing into the sea. Elliott and Manfrin then spotted a 'Jack' (Mitsubishi J2M3 Raiden), bracketing the Japanese fighter and making repeated runs until it too plunged into the sea. Ordered to return to their carrier, Elliott and Manfrin spotted what they identified as a 'Jill' (Nakajima B6N Tenzan) and promptly shot it down too.

A short while later squadronmate Lt Mulcahy spotted several 'Zekes' approaching the Task Force, and led his division in to attack them from the stern. However, when he pressed the gun button to open fire he found that his weapons had frozen. Breaking off his attack, Mulcahy ordered Ens Robert Pfeifer to take the lead. In only a few minutes Pfeifer managed to shoot down four 'Zekes'. Describing the combat in the squadron's Aircraft Action Report, Pfeifer recalled;

'I was not in the best position at the beginning of this run, so kicking a little right rudder, I shot a burst of tracers off to the Zeke's right and he immediately turned to port, putting me in a beautiful position for a shot from "seven o'clock above". I got in a long burst that struck the port wing and cockpit vicinity, and the aeroplane began to smoke, finally bursting into flames and crashing into the sea. I surprised another "Zeke", catching him about 50 ft off the water and hitting him from "six o'clock above". He immediately rolled over onto his back and then crashed into the sea. No fire or smoke was observed, and it is believed that the pilot was killed on this run, or that he lost control of his aeroplane in a desperate attempt to lose me.

'I then retired westward, with Lt(jg) Uthoff on my wing. I spotted another "Zeke" a few minutes later attempting to make a stern run on Uthoff. Uthoff and I weaved towards each other and I made a flat side run on the "Zeke", shooting from "two o'clock slightly above". Lt(jg) Uthoff observed the aeroplane to nose over and crash into the sea. Lt(jg) Uthoff made a head-on run on another "Zeke", and he got a short burst with no effect. Following Uthoff on this head-on run, I got in a long accurate burst from "twelve" to "two o'clock", hitting the aeroplane on the port side of the engine and cockpit. The engine and cockpit began to disintegrate and the aeroplane began to smoke and burn. It was last observed going into a sharp wingover to the left, before crashing into the water.

'I had closed to point blank range – approximately 30 ft – when firing at the last "Zeke", and after retiring to my carrier, I found my windshield and engine covered with human flesh, hair and blood stains.'

During the combat Lt(jg) Uthoff shot down two 'Zekes' as well, bringing VC-27's total for the day to 15 destroyed.

For the Fifth Air Force's fighter pilots, the invasion of the Philippines brought the first sustained air combat in several months. From 27 October 1944, when the first Fifth Air Force units arrived on Leyte, until early January 1945, when all but a few IJN and JAAF units had

withdrawn from the Philippines, USAAF fighter pilots claimed close to 700 Japanese aircraft shot down while covering the fighting on Leyte, Mindoro and Luzon. The first units to arrive on Leyte were the P-38-equipped 7th and 9th FSs of the 49th FG on 27 October – the 8th FS reached Tacloban three days later. The 475th FG's three squadrons moved to Leyte during November, the group taking up residence at Dulag, south of Tacloban, on 21 November. The 348th FG, with P-47s, did not complete its move to Leyte until early December. Once they arrived, the fighters were in action nearly every day.

Many of the Fifth Air Force's veteran fighter pilots added to their scores over the Philippines, the three top aces running their claims into double figures. Maj Thomas McGuire, CO of the 431st FS/475th FG, was the high scorer of the campaign with 14 victories. The 475th FG commander, Col Charles MacDonald, was next with 13 claims, followed by Maj Richard Bong with ten victories. Maj Gerald Johnson of the 49th FG was another of the veteran pilots who did well, claiming eight victories, including four in a day. The air battles provided opportunities for pilots who had not previously had the chance to score before to become aces. 1Lt Fernley Damstrom, who claimed eight victories flying with the 7th FS, was the highest scoring pilot among those who had not claimed any aerial victories prior to the Philippines. All told, no fewer than 25 USAAF pilots scored five or more victories during the Philippine campaign.

With the intensity of air combat and the larger numbers of conventional compared to kamikaze attacks, linking an individual ace's victories to a specific kamikaze attack is often problematical. Some claims, for example, were made on days when there were no kamikaze missions. However, given the division of target responsibilities between the JAAF and IJN Special Attack units, with the former concentrating on transport vessels while the IJN went after warships, it is highly probable, particularly in the aerial battles over Leyte, that a number of aces would have shot down kamikaze aircraft attempting to reach the transports lying just offshore. The majority of claims Fifth Air Force pilots submitted were for 'Oscars' and 'Zekes', which were the most commonly used kamikaze aircraft.

The first Fifth Air Force fighter units to arrive on Leyte were the 7th and 9th FSs of the 49th FG (Jack Lambert Collection, Museum of Flight)

There is a possibility that 1Lt Fernley Damstrom was the highest scoring Fifth Air Force pilot against the kamikaze during the Philippine campaign. Damstrom claimed his first aerial victory (an 'Oscar') on 2 November 1944, and followed this up with a 'Tojo' shot down on 11 November. Damstrom's best day was 7 December, which was also the Fifth Air Force's most successful day of aerial combat against the Japanese during the Philippine campaign. Ironically, it was the third anniversary of the Pearl Harbor attack too. That morning the US Army's 77th Infantry Division began landing south of Ormoc, on the west coast of Leyte.

Majs Richard Bong and Tommy McGuire, rivals for the position of leading Fifth Air Force ace. Bong and McGuire both added to their scores in the combats over the Philippines (US Air Force)

Unbeknownst to the Americans, the Imperial Japanese Army had also chosen that day to send a convoy to its beleaguered forces on Leyte. The JAAF and IJN sent aloft a strong fighter force to cover the convoy, and then to attack the American landing force once it had been identified, using both conventional and kamikaze attacks. In one of the largest kamikaze efforts of the campaign, the IJN sent out 21 kamikaze aircraft and the JAAF 23.

Among the squadrons sortied that day was the JAAF's Kinnou-tai Special Attack unit, which sent out ten Type 2 Two-Seat Fighters ('Nicks'). At around 0830 hrs that day, 1Lt Damstrom was leading a flight from the 7th FS on the 49th FG's second patrol over the Ormoc landing area when he saw a single 'Nick' flying 5000 ft below him. Damstrom dove down on the 'Nick' and set it on fire, claiming it destroyed. A little over an hour later, Damstrom and his wingman came across a formation of six 'Nicks' below them, heading towards the American landing. Diving down, Damstrom closed in on one of the twin-engined fighters and despatched it with two bursts. Later that afternoon he flew his second patrol over Ormoc Bay, where he claimed a 'Zeke' destroyed at 1430 hrs.

At 1220 hrs an IJN Special Attack unit had sent out eight Zero-sen kamikaze aircraft, with six more as escorts, from Mabalacat Field, in central Luzon. Shortly before Damstrom had made his final claim, the

A P-38 from the 475th Fighter Group lands at Tacloban in December 1944 – note the visiting FM-2s behind the fuel truck. Weather and construction difficulties delayed the transfer of the Fifth Air Force's fighter groups to Leyte (NARA 342FH-3A-30102)

460th FS/348th FG, with Maj William Dunham in the lead, sighted a formation of 13 aeroplanes flying below them off the northern tip of the island of Cebu, apparently on their way to Ormoc. Initially identifying the aircraft as 'Hamps' (A6M3s), Dunham and his pilots dived on the formation and the former quickly shot down two Zero-sens (and shortly thereafter claimed two 'Oscars'). The other 460th FS pilots claimed five more, these combats taking place at around 1400 hrs. It is possible that Damstrom's victory was over an aircraft from this formation that had escaped the onslaught of Dunham's P-47s.

Eight days later, on 15 December, Damstrom was leading one of two 7th FS flights patrolling over the landings on Mindoro Island when they came across a flight of seven Zero-sens at 0915 hrs. When attacked, the IJN fighters dived for the sea. Damstrom followed and managed to shoot one down. An hour later he came across another 'Zeke' flying just above the sea. Damstrom approached unseen and quickly shot down his second aircraft. As the Zero-sen rolled over, Damstrom saw bombs underneath the fuselage, so it may well have been a kamikaze aircraft. At 0645 hrs that morning, the 9th Kingotai had sent out 12 Zero-sens for a kamikaze attack on the transports lying off the Mindoro shore. It is possible, although not certain, that Damstrom's flight had run into this formation.

From 25 October 1944 (the date of the first Special Attack mission) through to 13 January 1945, the kamikaze pilots of the IJN and JAAF Shinbutai (Special Attack) units managed to hit around 137 ships, damaging many severely and causing 22 of them to sink or be scuttled due to the extent of the damaged inflicted. More than 2500 men were killed during the course of these attacks. The kamikaze proved to be more effective than conventional attacks, a post-war study estimating that on a per-sortie basis the kamikaze were seven to ten times more likely to hit their target, particularly as loss rates on conventional attacks remained greater than 50 per cent.

But the kamikaze attacks were costly. During the course of this campaign the IJN Special Attack units lost more than 400 aircraft, while the JAAF Special Attack units lost 700+. And conventional units within the JAAF and IJN also suffered severe losses during the fighting in the Philippines. By this stage of the war, experienced pilots (many of whom had volunteered for the Special Attack units) killed in kamikaze attacks simply could not be replaced.

Despite the damage they caused to Allied shipping, the kamikaze operations in the Philippines were in vain. The losses the kamikaze had inflicted on American and Allied forces were in no way crippling. The initial kamikaze attacks had not weakened the American carrier force, and the continuation of kamikaze attacks during the battle for the Philippines had not turned back the American invasion forces. Although the fighting would continue well into the summer of 1945, the Japanese had lost the Philippines. In January 1945 the remnants of the Special Attack and conventional units were withdrawn to Formosa to regroup.

Yet despite this failure, the losses of conventional aircraft and experienced pilots left the Japanese high command with little alternative to the employment of the Special Attack units as Japan's principal defensive weapon. When the next American blow fell, the kamikaze would lead the counterattack.

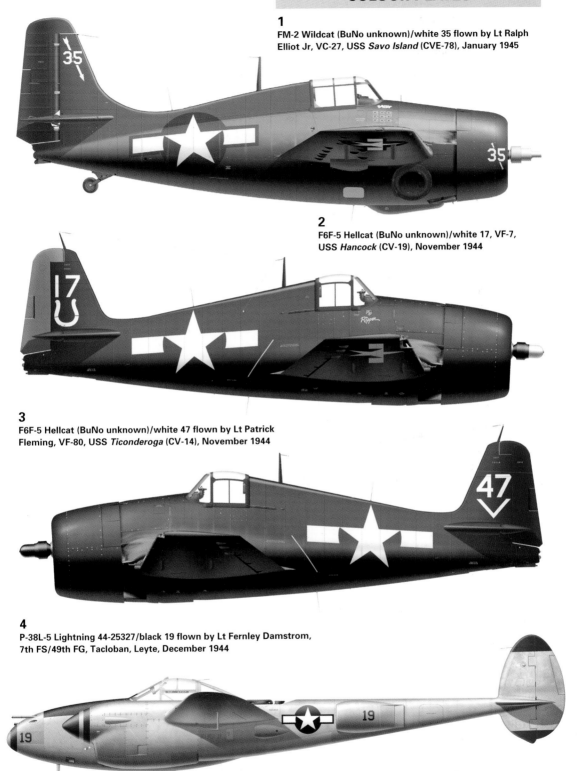

1
FM-2 Wildcat (BuNo unknown)/white 35 flown by Lt Ralph
Elliot Jr, VC-27, USS *Savo Island* (CVE-78), January 1945

2
F6F-5 Hellcat (BuNo unknown)/white 17, VF-7,
USS *Hancock* (CV-19), November 1944

3
F6F-5 Hellcat (BuNo unknown)/white 47 flown by Lt Patrick
Fleming, VF-80, USS *Ticonderoga* (CV-14), November 1944

4
P-38L-5 Lightning 44-25327/black 19 flown by Lt Fernley Damstrom,
7th FS/49th FG, Tacloban, Leyte, December 1944

23

5

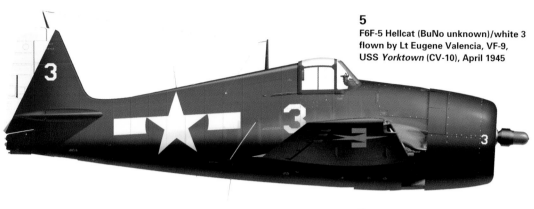

F6F-5 Hellcat (BuNo unknown)/white 3 flown by Lt Eugene Valencia, VF-9, USS *Yorktown* (CV-10), April 1945

6

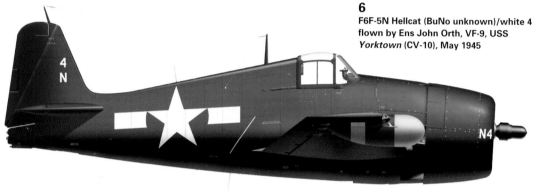

F6F-5N Hellcat (BuNo unknown)/white 4 flown by Ens John Orth, VF-9, USS *Yorktown* (CV-10), May 1945

7

F4U-1D Corsair (BuNo unknown)/white 66 flown by Ens Alfred Lerch, VF-10, USS *Intrepid* (CV-11), April 1945

8

F6F-5 Hellcat (BuNo unknown)/white 66 of VF/VBF-12, USS *Randolph* (CV-15), April-May 1945

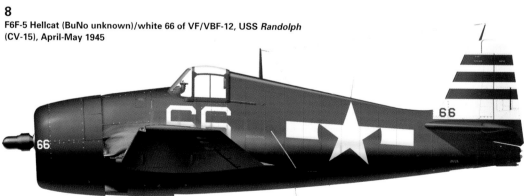

9
F6F-5 Hellcat (BuNo unknown)/white 35 flown by
Lt James Pearce, VF-17, USS *Hornet* (CV-12),
18-21 March 1945

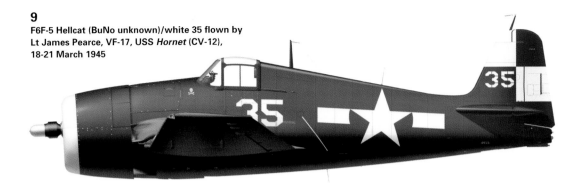

10
F6F-5 Hellcat BuNo 72748/white 33 flown by Lt(jg)
Willis Hardy, VF-17, USS *Hornet* (CV-12), 6 April 1945

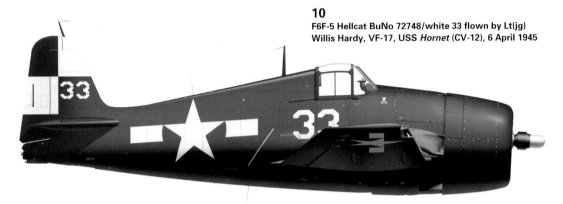

11
F6F-5 Hellcat (BuNo unknown)/white 10 of VF-30,
USS *Belleau Wood* (CVL-24), April 1945

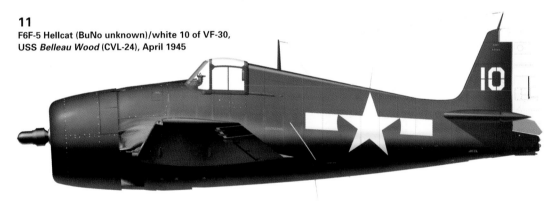

12
F6F-5 Hellcat BuNo 72522/blue 7 flown by Lt James
Cain, VF-45, USS *San Jacinto* (CVL-30), 23 March 1945

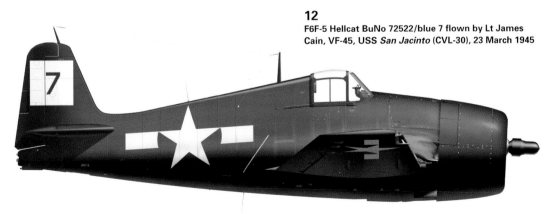

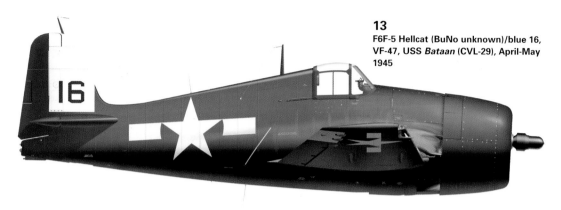

13
F6F-5 Hellcat (BuNo unknown)/blue 16, VF-47, USS *Bataan* (CVL-29), April-May 1945

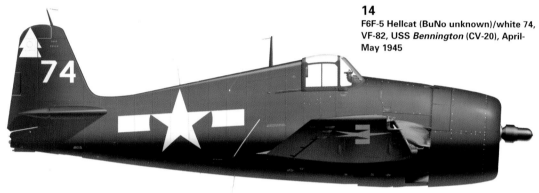

14
F6F-5 Hellcat (BuNo unknown)/white 74, VF-82, USS *Bennington* (CV-20), April-May 1945

15
F6F-5 Hellcat (BuNo unknown)/white 111 possibly flown by Lt Thaddeus Coleman, VF-83, USS *Essex* (CV-9), April-May 1945

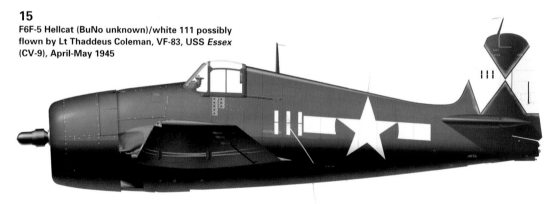

16
F6F-5 Hellcat (BuNo unknown)/white 126 of VF-83, USS *Essex* (CV-9), April-May 1945

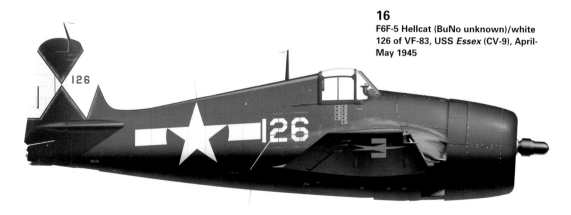

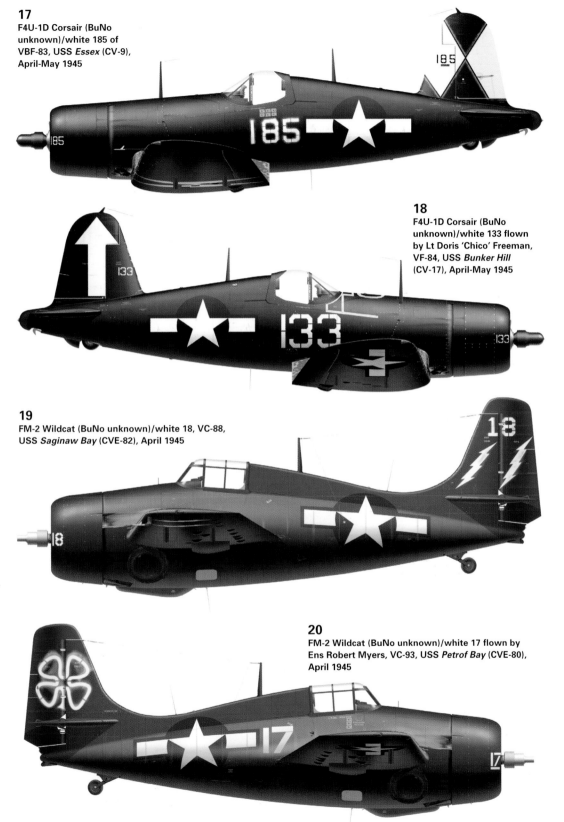

17
F4U-1D Corsair (BuNo
unknown)/white 185 of
VBF-83, USS *Essex* (CV-9),
April-May 1945

18
F4U-1D Corsair (BuNo
unknown)/white 133 flown
by Lt Doris 'Chico' Freeman,
VF-84, USS *Bunker Hill*
(CV-17), April-May 1945

19
FM-2 Wildcat (BuNo unknown)/white 18, VC-88,
USS *Saginaw Bay* (CVE-82), April 1945

20
FM-2 Wildcat (BuNo unknown)/white 17 flown by
Ens Robert Myers, VC-93, USS *Petrof Bay* (CVE-80),
April 1945

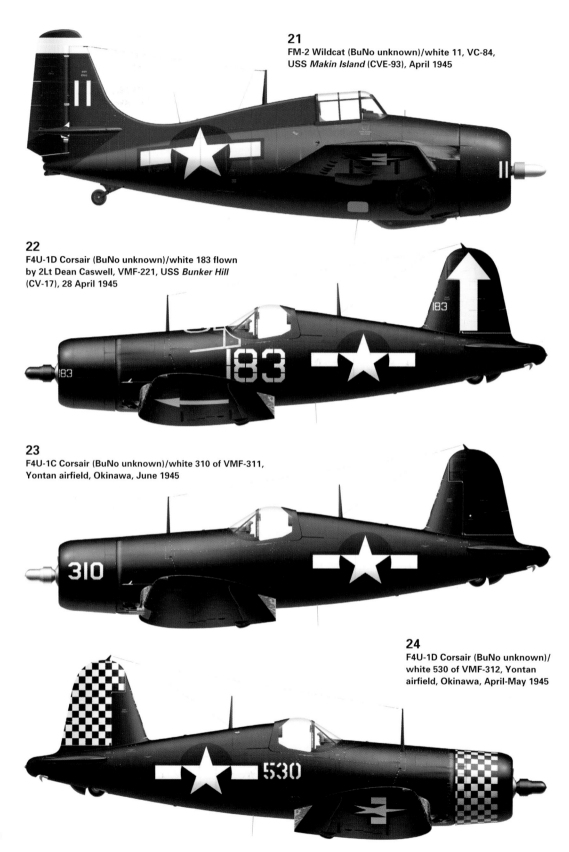

21
FM-2 Wildcat (BuNo unknown)/white 11, VC-84,
USS *Makin Island* (CVE-93), April 1945

22
F4U-1D Corsair (BuNo unknown)/white 183 flown
by 2Lt Dean Caswell, VMF-221, USS *Bunker Hill*
(CV-17), 28 April 1945

23
F4U-1C Corsair (BuNo unknown)/white 310 of VMF-311,
Yontan airfield, Okinawa, June 1945

24
F4U-1D Corsair (BuNo unknown)/
white 530 of VMF-312, Yontan
airfield, Okinawa, April-May 1945

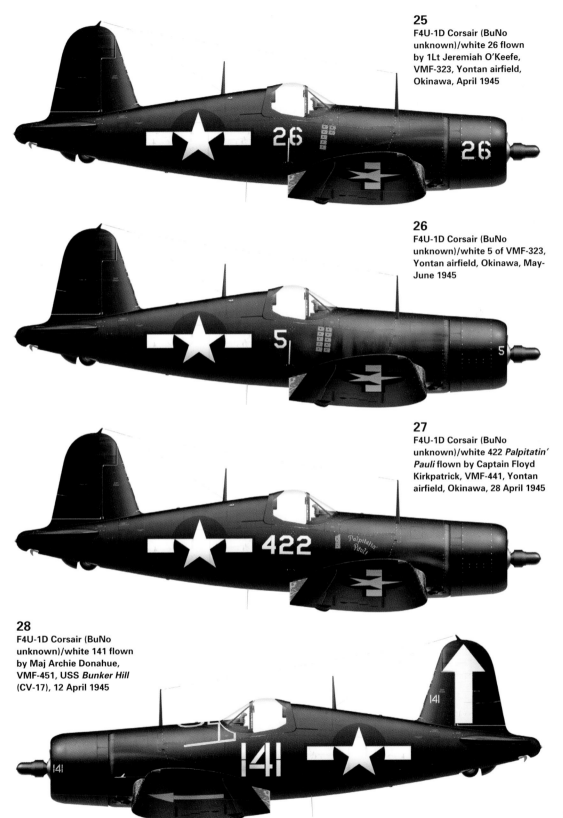

25
F4U-1D Corsair (BuNo unknown)/white 26 flown by 1Lt Jeremiah O'Keefe, VMF-323, Yontan airfield, Okinawa, April 1945

26
F4U-1D Corsair (BuNo unknown)/white 5 of VMF-323, Yontan airfield, Okinawa, May-June 1945

27
F4U-1D Corsair (BuNo unknown)/white 422 *Palpitatin' Pauli* flown by Captain Floyd Kirkpatrick, VMF-441, Yontan airfield, Okinawa, 28 April 1945

28
F4U-1D Corsair (BuNo unknown)/white 141 flown by Maj Archie Donahue, VMF-451, USS *Bunker Hill* (CV-17), 12 April 1945

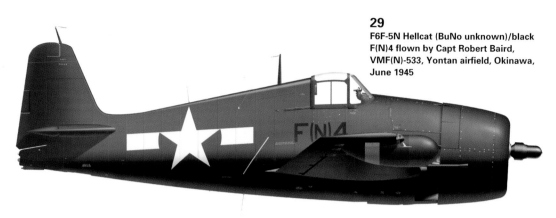

29
F6F-5N Hellcat (BuNo unknown)/black
F(N)4 flown by Capt Robert Baird,
VMF(N)-533, Yontan airfield, Okinawa,
June 1945

30
P-47N Thunderbolt, 44-87962/black 10 *BOTTOM'S UP* flown
by 1Lt William Mathis, 19th FS/318th FG, Ie Shima, May-
June 1945

31
P-47N Thunderbolt 44-87911/black 04 *DRINK'N SISTER* of Capt John Vogt,
19th FS/318th FG, Ie Shima, 28 May 1945

32
P-47N Thunderbolt 44-87959 flown by Capt Judge Wolfe, 333rd FS/318th FG,
Ie Shima, May-June 1945

OKINAWA – PRELUDE TO INVASION

The ultimate strategic objective for American forces in the Pacific was the isolation of Japan and the destruction of the Japanese military and industrial base through an assault on the home islands. After the capture of the Philippines, the next stage in the advance was to establish a forward base for the expected invasion of Japan. Staff studies in the autumn of 1944 focused on Okinawa, the principal island in the Ryukyu Island chain, as the most feasible objective given the resources available. From airfields on Okinawa USAAF bombers and fighters could strike at targets on Kyushu and Honshu, while the small islands just off the Okinawan coast offered a good anchorage for an invasion fleet.

On 3 October 1944, the American Joint Chiefs of Staff instructed Adm Chester Nimitz, Commander of the US Pacific Fleet and the Pacific Ocean Area, to seize positions in the Ryukyu Islands by 1 March 1945. Operation *Iceberg*, as the invasion of Okinawa was designated, was the largest amphibious assault of the Pacific War, involving more than half-a-million soldiers, sailors and airmen. The invasion force included more than 300 combat vessels and 1000 transport and auxiliary ships.

Due to the delay in the invasion of Luzon, and the prospect of poor weather during March, the date for the initial landings on Okinawa was moved to 1 April 1945.

Air support and air defence of the invasion fleet would be critical to the success of *Iceberg*. Until Marine Corps and USAAF aircraft could operate from airfields on Okinawa, the fleet would be vulnerable to air attack. Okinawa lay just 340 miles from Kyushu in the home islands, where the JAAF and IJN had more than 50 airfields between them. American planners had every expectation that the enemy would concentrate all available aircraft for the defence of Okinawa, and that kamikaze attacks would feature prominently in the Japanese response.

The Fast Carrier Task Force, now re-designated TF 58, would have to provide the main support for the invasion in the initial weeks of *Iceberg*, its aircraft striking at airfields on the home islands, providing air defence for the invasion fleet around Okinawa and CAS for troops on the ground. TF 58 consisted of 11 *Essex*-class fleet carriers and six *Independence*-class light carriers in four Task Groups (58.1, 58.2, 58.3 and 58.4), embarking 853 F6F-5 Hellcat and F4U-1D/FG-1D Corsair fighters in 24 US Navy and four Marine Corps squadrons. The fleet carriers now carried the increased complement of 70+ fighters as introduced in January 1945.

To provide additional close support TG 52.2 from the Amphibious Support Force had 18 escort carriers aboard which were embarked 345 FM-2 Wildcat and F6F-5 Hellcat fighters. In expectation of heavier air attacks the complement of fighters in the CVE composite squadrons had been increased from 16 to 20 or more.

As soon as practicable the Tenth Tactical Air Force, consisting of four Marine Air Groups (MAGs -31, -33, -22 and -14) with 12 squadrons of Corsairs and three nightfighter squadrons with F6F-5N Hellcats and the USAAF's 301st Fighter Wing with three fighter groups (318th, 413th and 507th FGs), would take over responsibility for air support and air defence from the US Navy.

There was no simple solution to the kamikaze threat. Experience in the Philippines had shown the kamikaze either had to be destroyed on the airfields they launched from or intercepted before they could reach the fleet. The US Navy's combat ships and transports were most vulnerable to surprise attack from small numbers of kamikaze that managed to elude the CAPs. As a defensive measure, the US Navy planned to establish a series of destroyer-based radar picket stations for early warning and fighter direction. These would be located around the island some 40 to 60 miles away from the invasion fleet anchorage.

With more fighters available from TF 58 and TG 52.2, and later from bases on Okinawa, a defence in greater depth could be provided, with CAPs over the picket ships at different altitudes and a CAP pool over the transport ships to draw on as needed. Although night carrier operations were difficult, for the dangerous dawn and dusk periods the larger *Essex*-class carriers were given a nightfighter detachment of four to six F6F-5Ns drawn from US Navy nightfighter squadrons that had been disbanded in the autumn of 1944.

The Japanese high command expected an attack on Okinawa as a precursor to the invasion of the home islands. In a rare show of inter-service cooperation, the JAAF and IJN agreed in January 1945 on a general outline of future operations, which was given official approval on 20 January. This plan, titled the 'Outline of Army and Navy Operations', called for the development of an inner defence perimeter, concentrated in the Ryukus. Once US forces had penetrated this zone, most likely through an attempt to capture Okinawa, JAAF and IJN forces would undertake a campaign of attrition to reduce the American quantitative superiority in ships and aircraft so as to delay as long as possible the invasion of Japan.

A contemporary news photograph purporting to show a JAAF Special Attack unit composed of recently trained university students taking their 'Oscar' fighters to the front (*Author's collection*)

There was little alternative to the adoption of Special Attack tactics as Japan's primary weapon. The outline plan called for the destruction of the American invasion fleet by Special Attack units, especially the carriers. The Japanese knew that the invasion force would have to rely on carrier-based aircraft for air support, and if these vessels could be eliminated, there was a chance the invasion would fail.

The plans developed stated categorically that 'Primary emphasis will be laid on the speedy activation, training and mass employment of air Special Attack units'. In the Philippines the kamikaze had operated in small numbers. The Japanese high command now planned kamikaze attacks en masse to overwhelm the US Navy's defences. For the first time, the JAAF and the IJN agreed to coordinate their attacks to maximise their effectiveness. Under the Ten-Go Operation Plan for the defence of the Ryukus, these combined attacks would be designated Kikusui (Floating Chrysanthemum, which was a reference to the Imperial Family's chrysanthemum symbol), and they would take place alongside conventional torpedo- and dive-bomber operations.

To prepare for the defence of Okinawa, the IJN reorganised its air units in Japan and concentrated them on bases in Kyushu, the southernmost of the major home islands. The IJN activated the Fifth Air Fleet in Kyushu to take over responsibility for operations under the new joint JAAF-IJN operating plan. Third Air Fleet units, flying from airfields on the Kanto plain in the defence of Honshu, were alerted to move to Kyushu on the activation of Operation Ten-Go, which called for ten mass kamikaze attacks. The Tenth Air Fleet was then activated on 1 March 1945 to take over command of new operational units converted from training groups, and it too would move to Kyushu on completion of training in Special Attack tactics. The combined strength of the Third, Fifth and Tenth Air Fleets would total some 3000 aircraft of all types by the beginning of April.

On 21 March 1945, the JAAF's Sixth Air Army, also in the process of moving to Kyushu, was placed under the command of the IJN, adding an additional 700+ aircraft in conventional and Special Attack units.

The difficulty facing both the JAAF and the IJN in their preparations for the defence of Japan was the shortage of new aircraft and the lack of trained pilots. With the decision to concentrate on kamikaze attacks, training standards were lowered even further in the belief that kamikaze pilots would need less than 100 flying hours to perform their mission. There was a belated recognition that the more experienced pilots and better aircraft would be more usefully employed in their conventional roles, or as escorts to the Special Attack units. It would fall to the least experienced pilots, flying obsolete aircraft, to perform the kamikaze attacks. Entire flying training classes in the JAAF and the IJN were 'asked' to volunteer for Special Attack units. Under intense social pressure, and with a strong sense of obligation to family and nation, most agreed. The IJN continued to form its Special Attack units by using personnel from its regular air groups, while the JAAF created dedicated and numbered Special Attack units.

In the battle for Okinawa the kamikaze pilots would be going up against US Navy, Marine Corps and USAAF pilots who were at the top of their game. Many of the division and flight leaders had been flying fighters for two years or more and were on their second combat tour. By the spring of 1945 many had accumulated more than 1000 flying hours in fighters. Most of the younger US Navy lieutenants and ensigns, and Marine Corps and USAAF lieutenants had significantly more flying hours than their Japanese counterparts. They were confident in their abilities, well versed in the tactics of aerial combat and flying superior aircraft. The few remaining Japanese veterans still posed a danger, but for the majority of the ill-trained conventional and kamikaze pilots, an encounter with American fighters typically ended in death.

PRE-INVASION STRIKES

On 14 March 1945, two weeks before the start of the Okinawa invasion, TF 58 sortied from its base at Ulithi for strikes against Japanese airfields on Kyushu (where the kamikaze units were based) and the remnants of the IJN fleet at Kure, on the Inland Sea. The initial strikes, scheduled for 18 March, would concentrate on the airfields around the Kanoya area, with additional strikes on airfields along Kyushu's east coast. Fighter sweeps would precede the main striking forces to eliminate any aerial opposition. The Japanese had been tracking the progress of TF 58 toward Kyushu for several days, but were unsure if this was a precursor to an invasion or a more limited strike against the airfields. The Fifth Air Fleet planned to send out Special Attack units to strike at TF 58 and to intercept aircraft attacking the airfields, but the Combined Fleet headquarters gave instructions for it not to employ the full force unless a landing was imminent.

At around 0530 hrs on 18 March, TF 58's four Task Groups began launching the first strikes. The F6F-5 Hellcats of VF-17, flying off USS *Hornet* (CV-12), were tasked with conducting one of the first fighter sweeps over Kanoya airfield. Squadron CO Lt Cdr Marshall Beebe led 20 Hellcats on the mission. Over southern Kyushu VF-17 ran into several flights of Zero-sen fighters, likely from the 203rd Kokutai, based in the area. Crossing Kagoshima Bay en route to the airfield, one of

In preparation for the strikes on the Kyushu airfields, TF 58 had white bands painted on the cowlings of all of its F6Fs and F4Us. These Hellcats from VF-17, on board USS *Hornet*, are in the process of having these markings applied (*NARA 80G-314320*)

Beebe's division leaders, Lt(jg) Thomas Harris, spotted a 'Zeke' flying below him and dove down after it. Lts Bob Coats and Willis Parker took their divisions to act as cover. Using an altitude advantage, three Zero-sen fighters attacked Parker's division. Parker shot down a 'Zeke' in a head-on attack. Coats saw a second 'Zeke' making a run on Parker, but he managed to slide in behind the fighter unseen and set it on fire for his first victory of the day.

Losing sight of Harris' division, Coats and Parker continued on towards Kanoya airfield for a strafing attack. Approaching the target, they were descending to 8000 ft when a formation of five 'Zekes' was spotted 1000 ft above them in their 'six o'clock' position. Quickly reversing course, Coats and Parker approached the formation from behind at the 'five o'clock' position, climbing at maximum power. The 'Zekes' were flying in a tight echelon formation. As the Hellcats approached, one of the IJN fighters dived away, possibly to act as a decoy.

While Parker kept his division above as cover, Coats led his division into the attack on the remaining four 'Zekes'. His wingman, Ens Geremiah Foster, fired on the fighter on the right of the formation, shooting it down. Coats then took on the other three aircraft and, in quick succession, shot them down. Working from right to left, he closed to point blank range before firing three short bursts. One 'Zeke' exploded and the other two fell away in flames. Flying out to the rendezvous point after the action, Lt Coats saw a Corsair with two 'Zekes' on its tail. He attacked the fighter closest to the Corsair, hitting it in the starboard wing and watching as the pilot bailed out. Coats, who had two previous victories from a tour with VF-18, had become an 'ace in a day' – the first of 20 pilots to achieve this distinction during the Okinawa campaign.

Lt Cdr Beebe, meanwhile, had led his other two divisions – joined by Lt(jg) Harris' division – in a strafing attack on Kanoya airfield, where they claimed six aeroplanes destroyed on the ground. As the two divisions were pulling up from their strafing run, they were attacked by a force of ten to fifteen fighters that they later identified as 'Zekes' and Ki-84 'Franks'. Beebe, who had climbed up to establish a rendezvous orbit, found himself in the midst of a general melee, with 'Zekes', 'Franks' and Hellcats going around in a circle. Beebe attacked a 'Zeke' in the circle and shot it down. He then saw another 'Zeke' on the tail of Lt(jg) Tilman Pool, who had himself just shot down a 'Zeke' for his first aerial victory. Beebe moved in quickly and shot down his second 'Zeke' of the day.

Beebe and Pool then pulled out and headed south, only for the latter pilot to come under attack from a 'Frank' that dived on him from above and astern. Beebe turned and made a head-on attack on the Ki-84, the two aircraft firing at each other and closing to 200 ft. Beebe managed to set the 'Frank' on fire, the JAAF fighter flashing past him before crashing into Kagoshima Bay. Heading south once again with other VF-17 pilots, Beebe encountered another 'Frank' that turned into him to avoid another Hellcat's attack. Beebe fired and sent his fourth aircraft down into the bay. In his final combat Beebe caught yet another 'Frank', knocking off a section of its port wing and starting a fire in the fuselage. This fighter, too, crashed into Kagoshima Bay for Beebe's fifth victory of the day, making him the second 'ace in a day' of the campaign. Lt(jg) Pool managed to shoot down a second 'Zeke' and claim a third as a probable.

Pilots of VF-82 aboard *Bennington* get a briefing prior to participating in the first strikes against Kyushu on 18 March 1945. The first day's strikes targeted airfields in the southern part of Kyushu (*NARA 80G-306429*)

In total, VF-17's pilots claimed 32 fighters shot down that morning.

TF 58 flew a series of strikes against the Kyushu airfields during the course of the day, claiming 124 aircraft shot down and 275 destroyed on the ground. On one of the afternoon sweeps three divisions of F4U-1D Corsairs from VBF-83, flying off *Essex*, ran into a large formation of 25 to 30 Japanese fighters, which they identified as 'Zekes', off the east coast of Kyushu as they were withdrawing from strikes on Karasahara, Waifu, Kumomoto and Tomitaka airfields.

The leader of the third division, Lt James Stevens, had been hit by AAA on one of the airfield attacks. His Corsair was trailing smoke as the formation crossed the coast just as the 'Zekes' attacked. Lt Thomas Reidy, leading the formation, ordered his pilots to defend Stevens, and for the next 15 minutes the Corsair pilots of VBF-83 put up a desperate fight to protect him as they slowly moved the formation out to sea towards a rescue submarine. Following their tactical doctrine, the pilots from VBF-83 kept their speed up to 180 knots or more, finding that at these higher speeds they could manoeuvre with the attacking 'Zekes'. Using protective weaves, the Corsair pilots managed to keep the IJN fighters off their tails and, in the process, claim ten of them destroyed, four probably destroyed and two damaged. Lt Reidy, a former Helldiver pilot with VB-83 who had joined VBF-83 on its formation in January 1945, claimed his first two victories in this action. Sadly, Lt Stevens ditched his Corsair but was never found.

It appears that VMF-221, flying Corsairs off USS *Bunker Hill* (CV-17), also ran into this formation of 25-30 'Zekes' and 'Franks' as they were withdrawing past Tomitaka airfield at around the same time. On seeing the enemy fighters, Capt William Snider led his three divisions into the attack, and he and his wingman subsequently destroyed four aircraft during the ensuing combat. Snider first fired at a 'Frank' that was attacking him head-on, setting it on fire. He then attacked a second Ki-84 from a position above and to the rear of the enemy fighter. The JAAF pilot took no evasive action, choosing instead to bail out when Snider set his fighter on fire. Snider's third kill was a 'Zeke' attacking another Corsair. Approaching from the 'four o'clock' position, Snider opened fire and the 'Zeke' burst into flames.

The leader of VMF-221's third division, Capt John Delancey, after making a run on a Zero-sen, pulled up to find himself in the midst of a formation of 'Zekes' and 'Franks', with another 'Zeke' directly in front of him, two on his tail and his radio inoperative. Fortunately for Delancey, his wingman, 2Lt Dean Caswell, was there to shoot one of the IJN fighters off his tail, while Delancey despatched the 'Zeke' in front of him. Moving down the coast towards the sea, Caswell then came across

An F4U-1D from VBF-83 returns from one of the strikes over Kyushu. VBF-83 claimed 18 aircraft shot down during the operation on 18 March (*Robert Lawson Collection, NMNA*)

two more 'Zekes' and managed to shoot down both of them from the 'six o'clock' position for his first combat victories.

VMF-221's Aircraft Action Report commented on the poor quality of the Japanese fighters, noting that the '"Franks" and "Zekes" did not use their natural advantages to any extent – even their turns were wide and sloppy. Their speed and dives were inferior, and their only manoeuvre seemed to be the split-S'.

IJN vessels in the Inland Sea were the main targets for the next day, 19 March. TGs 58.1, 58.3 and 58.4 were assigned to attack the main IJN base at Kure, where photo-reconnaissance on 18 March had identified the super battleship *Yamato*, the battleship *Haruna* and three light carriers in port, while the air groups from TG 58.2 would attack naval vessels in the harbour at Kobe, near Osaka. Fighter sweeps went in to clear the way for the Helldivers and Avengers.

On the way to Kure the strike forces would pass near the airfield at Matsuyama, on the island of Shikoku, which was home to the 343rd Kokutai. The 343rd had been established at the end of 1944 under the command of Capt Minoru Genda (of Pearl Harbor fame) as an elite unit composed of some of the IJN's last remaining expert fighter pilots and equipped with the latest and most capable naval fighter, the Kawanishi N1K2-J Shiden-Kai ('George'). Genda hoped that his new unit would go some way to winning back air superiority over the American carrier fighters. 19 March 1945 would be the 343rd Kokutai's first opportunity for combat.

At 0618 hrs 20 F6F-5 Hellcats from VBF-17 took off from *Hornet* to join 16 Corsairs from VMF-123 flying off USS *Bennington* (CV-20) for a sweep over the airfields in the area around Kure. Upon reaching the rendezvous point, Lt Edwin Conant, leading VBF-17's aeroplanes that morning, found that VMF-123 had gone on ahead. Flying west of Shikoku toward Kure just above an overcast, Conant saw 40 aircraft approaching his formation. These were from the 343rd Kokutai's Squadrons 407 and 701, and they immediately attacked the Hellcats.

For the next 25 minutes the pilots of VBF-17 fought desperately against the Japanese fighters, who they later described as 'exceedingly aggressive', with good organisation, discipline and tactics. Unfamiliar

An F4U-1D Corsair of VBF-84 aboard *Bunker Hill* prepares to take off for the strikes on the IJN base at Kure on 19 March (*NARA 80G-312608*)

Kanoya East airfield is attacked by aircraft from Air Group 82 on 18 March 1945. Fighter sweeps went in first to clear the skies of enemy fighters. Forty minutes later the TBM Avengers and SB2C Helldivers came in to pound the airfields (*NARA Bennington After Action Report for 18 March 1945*)

with the 'George', many of the VBF-17 pilots mistook the fighter for other types. For example, Conant claimed two 'Franks' shot down, while Lt(jg) Byron Eberts, a future VBF-17 ace, claimed two 'Georges' and a 'Tony', getting his first N1K2-J in a head-on run, and shooting the other aircraft off the tails of fellow pilots. Two more future aces, Ens Robert Clark and Harold Yeremian, claimed two aircraft each. In the confusion the pilots of VBF-17 claimed 25 Japanese fighters destroyed, but at the cost of six of their own pilots shot down. It seems that Squadrons 407 and 701 lost four pilots in the battle with VBF-17.

Several other future aces had run-ins with the Shiden-Kais of the 343rd Kokutai that morning. Several divisions from VF-83, flying off *Essex*, were sent on an early morning sweep over Matsuyama West airfield. A warning to the leader of Squadron 407 that American aeroplanes were approaching the base brought 16 Shiden-Kais over Matsuyama just as the Hellcats of VF-83 made their first pass over the field. A swirling dogfight developed, and in the melee Lt(jg)s Hugh Batten and Samuel Brocato both claimed two fighters shot down, which they identified as 'Jacks' (Mitsubishi J3M Raiden).

Four divisions of Hellcats from VF-9, off USS *Yorktown* (CV-10), returning from a strike on the airfield at Kure, descended to strafe the airfield at Saijo on the northwest coast of Shikoku and then turned towards Matsuyama airfield. En route, Lt Bert Eckard's division ran into eight to ten Shiden-Kais belonging to the 343rd Kokutai's Squadron 301 just after 0810 hrs. A running fight quickly developed, during which the division constantly used a defensive weave. Lt Naoshi Kanno attacked Eckard's Hellcat but overshot his target. Eckard then got in a 15-degree deflection shot at what he identified as a 'Frank', setting Kanno's Shiden-Kai on fire and forcing him to bail out. Ens Joseph Kaelin, Eckard's wingman, saw a fighter on the tail of another Hellcat and promptly shot down the Shiden Kai of CPO Yasuharu Nikko, who crashed and was killed. Kaelin claimed this as a 'Zeke', and added a probable that he identified as a 'Tojo' and another 'Zeke' damaged.

An F6F-5 Hellcat from VF-9 runs into the barrier rigged up across the flightdeck of *Yorktown* upon its return from the first strikes on Kyushu (*NARA 80G-328318*)

An hour later, 16 Hellcats from VF-17 approached Kure on a combined bombing and fighter sweep just before the attack on the IJN ships in the harbour. As they neared the target they could see that the sky over the city was alive with anti-aircraft fire, the multi-coloured explosions creating a rainbow of colour over the Japanese fleet below. Shore batteries and the warships were throwing up a barrage more intense than anything the attacking US Navy pilots had ever seen. Watching the two divisions ahead of him, Lt Jim Pearce, leading the third division, was not sure how they could survive diving into the maelstrom of fire.

He was about to dive on the vessels when Lt Thomas Harris, leading the fourth division, called out a large group of enemy fighters on the right. This proved to be a mixed formation of JAAF 'Oscar' and 'Frank' fighters attempting to intercept the American aircraft. Pearce led the two Hellcat divisions in the direction on the Japanese aircraft, catching a 'Frank' as it tried to split-S. The JAAF fighter exploded when hit by Pearce's fire. He then attacked another 'Frank', which started to trail smoke prior to it being finished off by a second Hellcat.

By then Lt Harris had run into another group of aircraft, making a head-on run at a 'Tony' which exploded. He then saw two 'Zekes' above and behind him. Reversing course, Harris pulled his Hellcat almost straight up behind one of the IJN fighters and hit it in the engine and the cockpit. Moments later the 'Zeke' fell away in flames.

During the same action squadronmate Lt(jg) Tilman Pool shot down a 'Frank' for his third kill in two days.

An F4U-1D Corsair from VF-6 escorts two VB-6 SB2C Helldivers past a Japanese airfield during the 19 March strikes on Kure (*NARA RG 208AA-Box 249-Folder H-42141FN*)

Later that afternoon VF-17's Lt Bob Coats narrowly missed becoming an 'ace in a day' for the second day running when, leading a division of three Hellcats, he ran into small formations of Japanese aircraft. Coats claimed a probable 'Zeke' on his own, a third of a 'George' shot down with the other two pilots in his division and a third of probable kills on two 'Tonys' and four 'Zekes'. During the day's actions US Navy pilots claimed 80 Japanese aeroplanes destroyed, 26 probably destroyed and 16 damaged.

Although ordered to respond to the American attacks with only minimal forces unless a landing was imminent, Vice-Adm Ugaki had nevertheless ordered that both conventional and Special Attack units were to immediately target the American carriers. On 18 March USS *Enterprise* (CV-6) was hit with a dud bomb, a 'Betty' bomber narrowly missed *Intrepid* and *Yorktown* was struck by a bomb that exploded near the ship's side. At the end of the day Japanese pilots reported that one large American carrier had been sunk and two more had been set on fire. The next day conventional bomb attacks hit USS *Wasp* (CV-18) and *Franklin*. *Wasp* managed to effect repairs, but *Franklin* was severely damaged and knocked out of the war. Again, Japanese reports were overly optimistic, claiming a second carrier sunk and another set on fire.

Encouraged by these apparent successes Vice-Adm Ugaki ordered the 721st Kokutai Jinrai Butai (Thunder God Corps) with its Ohka piloted rocket bombs to attack an American carrier force that was then withdrawing from the waters off Japan. Despite lacking adequate fighter

An F6F-5 Hellcat of VF-17 over Kure on 19 March. US Navy and Marine Corps pilots were astounded at the volume of flak the ships in the harbour sent up to greet them, and the array of colours created when the shells exploded. The latter created a beautiful, but deadly, pattern in the sky (*Jack Lambert Collection, Museum of Flight*)

escorts, the bombers were ordered aloft. Shortly before noon on 21 March a force of 18 'Betty' bombers took off from Kanoya airfield. Fifteen of them were carrying Ohka rocket bombs, the pilots of which had all written farewell letters to their families prior to leaving. The escort started out with 55 Zero-sens, but no fewer than 25 of them had to return to base due to mechanical faults.

Lt Jim Pearce had been on CAP over TG 58.1 for two hours with his own division from VF-17 and a second division from VBF-17, led by Lt(jg) Henry Mitchell, when he received a radio call. Radar had picked up a large formation of aircraft 70 miles away at an altitude of 13,000 ft. The fighter director said 'Gate', meaning intercept at full throttle. Pearce immediately climbed to 18,000 ft so as to give his two divisions a height advantage. As he came within ten miles of the Japanese force, Pearce could make out 18 'Betty' bombers flying in a 'V of Vs' formation, with a fighter escort above. He ordered Mitchell to spread out so that they could simultaneously attack both sides of the Japanese formation.

As they neared the bombers, Pearce had a flash of recognition that his approach was just like the high side runs he had made in gunnery training. As they closed with the approaching 'Bettys', the two divisions did a 180-degree turn so as to come out in the same direction. As they descended, Pearce radioed 'Forget the fighters, let's go after the bombers'.

He fired at one 'Betty' at the rear of the formation, getting hits on the vital fuel tanks between the engine and the fuselage and setting the big bomber on fire. Pearce descended to come up underneath his next target, and to his astonishment he saw that the 'Betty' was carrying a small aeroplane. He opened fire, and as the bomber started burning the Ohka broke loose. Pearce later recalled a chaotic scene of 'Bettys' on fire, Ohkas falling away and Hellcats diving in to take on a new target, or to shoot up a bomber that had already been hit.

Pearce received credit for two 'Bettys', while element leader Lt(jg) Murray Winfield claimed 4.5 bombers shot down. The high-scorer for

Lt Jim Pearce led the VF-17 and VBF-17 divisions that were the first to intercept the 721st Kokutai formation. Pearce claimed two 'Bettys' destroyed (*Museum of Flight*)

Despite an insufficient number of escorting fighters, the 721st Kokutai Jinrai Butai sent off 15 'Betty' bombers carrying Ohka piloted rocket bombs to attack the American fleet. Here, the 'Betty' crews sit waiting for the order to take off (*NHHC NH-73100*)

the *Hornet* divisions was Lt(jg) Henry Mitchell, who was given credit for five 'Bettys', making him an 'ace in a day'.

Just as VF-17's two divisions attacked the Japanese formation, two divisions from VF-30, flying off the light carrier USS *Belleau Wood* (CVL-24), joined in. Ens James Reber, flying wing on Lt(jg) Harvey Sturdevant, joined his leader in attacking the 'Betty' formation, claiming two shot down. Soon separated from his leader, Reber went after a 'Zeke' that he saw at 'ten o'clock'. Pulling in behind the fighter, he fired a burst that hit the 'Zeke's' wings and fuselage, setting it on fire. He then saw another 'Zeke' at 'nine o'clock'. Again pulling in behind the IJN machine, he fired a burst into the fuselage and engine. The 'Zeke' exploded with such force that debris damaged Reber's engine.

With a 'Dinah' shot down in February and two 'Zekes' destroyed on 18 March, Reber's four claims of the day made him an ace. Lt(jg) Sturdevant also did well, claiming two 'Zekes' and a 'Betty'. In total, VF-30 pilots were credited with 11 'Zekes' and ten 'Betty' bombers destroyed. Between them, VF-17 and VF-30 claimed a total of 26 'Bettys' – more than were actually on the mission! The day became known as the 'First Turkey Shoot' in VF-30's squadron history.

After the strikes on Kyushu and the Inland Sea, TF 58 switched to attacking targets on Okinawa and the surrounding islands in preparation for the invasion. On 28 and 29 March (four days before the main landings on Okinawa) TGs 58.3 and 58.4 returned to conduct sweeps over the airfields on Kyushu. Combined Fleet headquarters was aware that an invasion of Okinawa was imminent and decided not to counter these sweeps, preferring to conserve aeroplanes for the initiation of Operation *Ten-Go*. Nevertheless, US Navy and Marine Corps fighter pilots claimed 36 aircraft shot down over the two days.

Assigned to sweep the airfields around Kagoshima and the JAAF base at Chiran on the western side of Kagoshima Bay, 20 F4U Corsairs from VF-10 came across a formation of eight Japanese fighters heading for Kanoya airfield. Lt(jg) Philip Kirkwood was ordered to take his division down to intercept them. Using repeated high-side runs, the division claimed six of the eight fighters. Kirkwood, who had scored four victories during 1944, claimed two 'Zekes' to make ace.

Between 18 and 29 March 1945, US Navy and Marine Corps carrier pilots had claimed 332 Japanese aeroplanes destroyed in the air. Most of these aircraft appear to have been from conventional units, although 69 Special Attack aeroplanes were sent out to attack the American fleet. The combined JAAF and IJN losses amounted to 161 aeroplanes – 83 per cent of the aircraft committed. The extensive damage inflicted on Japanese airfield installations duly prevented the Fifth Air Fleet from undertaking major actions for several weeks.

The Ohka-carrying 'Bettys' were sitting ducks for the Hellcats of VF-17 and VF-30. This gun camera film shows one of the bombers coming under attack. The wings of the piloted rocket bomb can just be seen under the 'Betty's' belly (*NARA 80G-185585*)

THE APRIL BATTLES

When American troops began landing on Okinawa on the morning of 1 April 1945, JAAF and IJN forces were not ready to initiate the Ten-Go air operation, despite the Combined Fleet having issued an invasion alert a week earlier. The Fifth Air Fleet was still recovering from the losses it had recently received, while the Third Air Fleet and Sixth Air Army, which had 25 Special Attack units to deploy, were still moving their squadrons to Kyushu. Many of the Tenth Air Fleet's Special Attack units were still undergoing training.

With the invasion confirmed through reconnaissance flights, the Tenth Air Fleet was nonetheless ordered to move its units to Kanoya. The IJN air units were assigned responsibility for attacking the American warships, particularly the carriers, while JAAF assets attacked the invasion transports. The movement of aircraft and personnel to bases on Kyushu took time, so a massed attack on the American invasion fleet had to be delayed. In the interim, JAAF and IJN units mounted daily reconnaissance flights with 'Dinah' and 'Myrt' aircraft in an effort to find and track the American carriers and initiate attacks on the invasion force with conventional aircraft and small numbers of kamikaze.

Shortly after noon on 3 April, two 'Myrts' returned from a reconnaissance mission and reported that they had sighted a group of American ships 80 miles off the island of Amami Shima, in the Ryukyu chain north of Okinawa. The Fifth Air Fleet ordered a combined attack, sending off 20 conventional 'Judys' and 24 kamikaze aircraft, which included six more 'Judys' and eight Zero-sen fighters, at 1500 hrs. The attacking force had an escort of 32 Zero-sens and eight Shiden-Kai fighters. The Sixth Air Army despatched 35 aeroplanes – the 18 kamikaze that took off that afternoon may have been included in this figure. The 23rd Special Attack unit sent out five 'Sonias', which were joined by seven more from two other units, and six 'Tonys' from the 105th Fighter Regiment, which had been converted into a Special Attack unit.

That afternoon ten of VF-83's Hellcats were sent off to search for Japanese shipping between Kyushu and Okinawa. The pilots found no vessels, but on their return flight they ran into Japanese aircraft heading down the island chain toward Okinawa and the fleet. Flying near the Amami Islands, Ens Lawrence Clark and his wingman spotted a 'Judy' just above the water. Diving down, Clark fired a burst at the aircraft in a 35-degree deflection shot, which hit the engine and set the dive-bomber on fire. Moments later it crashed into the sea. Within minutes they had also encountered a 'Val', which Clark promptly shot down.

Hearing calls from nearby friendly fighters, Clark flew to help, running into two 'Tonys' on the way. Making head-on passes, Clark and his wingman shot down one each.

Lt Thaddeus Coleman and his wingman, Ens Richard Langdon, were returning from their sector search when they spotted seven 'Sonias' – most likely part of the JAAF kamikaze force – flying near the Osumi Island group. Coleman noticed that each 'Sonia' was carrying a bomb

On 3 April Lt Thaddeus Coleman of VF-83 shot down four 'Sonias' to become an ace. He would claim eight Japanese aircraft during the Okinawa campaign, getting six kills in only two missions (*via the author*)

underneath its fuselage. When the 'Sonias' spotted the approaching Hellcats they jettisoned their bombs and tried to flee. Coleman and Langdon attacked repeatedly, Coleman shooting down four aircraft and Langdon the remaining three. With two previous kills with VF-6, and a claim for a 'Frank' on 31 March, Coleman became an ace with these victories. The pattern of scoring multiple kills in a single mission would occur frequently in the weeks to come, and particularly three days later.

KIKUSUI NO 1 – 6-7 APRIL 1945

On 6 April the Japanese launched the first of ten massed kamikaze attacks on the American fleet off Okinawa – Kikusui Operation No 1. The first kamikaze began taking off between 1015 hrs and 1310 hrs. By the end of the day the IJN had sent out 230 kamikaze aircraft and the JAAF 130. More than 130 IJN and JAAF fighters accompanied the kamikaze as escorts, with IJN dive-bombers adding their weight to the attack.

Nineteen US Navy and four Marine Corps carrier squadrons engaged the Japanese in running battles that began around noon and lasted into the early evening. American pilots claimed 275 Japanese aircraft shot down – the fourth highest one-day total of the war. Thirteen pilots became aces that day, including four who were 'aces in a day', shooting down five or more aeroplanes. Ten pilots shot down four aircraft and a further 17 shot down three. Honours for the day went to the pilots of VF-83 and sister-squadron VBF-83, who claimed 69 aircraft. VF-30 was the next highest scoring squadron, claiming 47 aircraft shot down.

The day began with reconnaissance flights by two 'Myrts' and a JAAF 'Dinah', which located two groups of American carriers south of the island of Oshima. Later that morning 23 conventional 'Judys' took off to attack these carrier groups. The Shinrai Butai Special Attack unit of the Dai San Kenbutai from the 721st Kokutai sent out 18 Zero-sen kamikaze, while seven 'Judys' from the No 210 Butai Suisei-tai joined

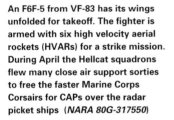

An F6F-5 from VF-83 has its wings unfolded for takeoff. The fighter is armed with six high velocity aerial rockets (HVARs) for a strike mission. During April the Hellcat squadrons flew many close air support sorties to free the faster Marine Corps Corsairs for CAPs over the radar picket ships (*NARA 80G-317550*)

them. This formation appears to have run into two division from VF-83 and two from VBF-83, which were on a CAP over TG 58.3.

Lt Thaddeus Coleman, who was flying with VF-83's second division, was vectored toward the island of Tokuna Shima. At around 1230 hrs he saw two bogeys ahead of him flying at 3000 ft coming out of the overcast. Dropping their belly tanks, Coleman and his wingman went to full power and chased the aircraft, which were identified as two 'Judys'. Coleman went below one of them, pulled his nose up and fired a burst into the 'Judy's' starboard wing, causing it to fall off to the left. He then fired another burst into the port wing of the second 'Judy', which exploded. Chasing after the first Judy, Coleman caught up with it weaving just above the sea. A short burst to the engine sent the aircraft crashing into the water.

The four VF-83 and VBF-83 divisions claimed nine 'Zekes', an 'Oscar' and three 'Judys' during the combat. The Aircraft Action report noted that the Japanese aircraft 'maintained no formation and tried no effective evasive tactics'.

The main combats took place after noon. Beginning around 1230 hrs, groups of kamikaze and their escorting fighters began taking off from airfields in Kyushu and heading south. It was hoped that the waves of attackers would overwhelm the American defences. Among the aircraft the IJN Special Attack units sent out were 'Val' dive-bombers (38 from the Usa-Ku, Dai-Ichi Seito-tai and the Nagoya-tai), obsolete 'Kates' (14 from the Usa-Ku and 13 from the Himeiji-Ku units) and 'Jills' and older A6M2 versions of the Zero-sen. The JAAF's 22nd, 36th, 37th, 38th, 43rd, 44th, 62nd and 73rd Tokubetsu-tai contributed 'Oscars', 'Sonias' and obsolete 'Nates', while eight 'Franks' came from the 101st and 102nd Fighter Sentai. The presence of three aircraft with fixed landing gear – 'Vals', 'Sonias' and 'Nates' – appears to have caused problems with aircraft recognition amongst the American pilots, who claimed more than 100 'Vals' shot down for the day but only four 'Sonias' and no 'Nates'.

VF-83 had sent out three divisions of Hellcats and VBF-83 two divisions of Corsairs on a long-range search for enemy shipping near Amami Shima and Tokuna Shima. In the early afternoon they ran into Japanese aircraft heading south toward Okinawa in small formations – 'Vals', 'Judys' and 'Kates' with a Zero-sen escort and four 'Sonias' with an escort of eight 'Tonys' – encountering more than 50 aeroplanes. Between 1430 and 1600 hrs the pilots of the two squadrons claimed 32 of them shot down.

VF-83's Ens William Kingston, who would become an ace six days later, was flying in Lt David Robinson's division when it ran into several formations of 'Vals', one after another. Kingston claimed three dive-bombers shot down prior to his guns jamming. Breaking out of cloud, he then saw another 'Val' directly below him. Managing to clear his guns, Kingston downed the aircraft in an attack from above.

Leading the second section in Lt Thomas Conder's division, Ens Lawrence Clark and his wingman Ens Norm Berube had an encounter with the 'Zeke' escort which proved that even at this late stage in the war no Zero-sen pilot could be taken for granted. Hearing a cry for help from friendly aircraft, Condor turned his division toward the call and, climbing for altitude, ran into a formation of four 'Sonias'. Each pilot in

Lt(jg) Hugh Batten was awarded the Navy Cross for his actions on 6 April, when he and his wingman, Lt(jg) Samuel Brocato, shot down eight 'Zekes' from a formation of nine kamikazes. Both pilots became aces that day (*via the author*)

A damaged F6F-5 of VF-30 on board the *Belleau Wood* after a mission. VF-30 pilots claimed 47 Japanese aircraft shot down during the first Kikusui kamikaze attack on 6 April (*NARA 80G-320274*)

the division took one and shot it down. This was Clark's fifth kill, making him an ace. Climbing through the overcast, the division saw four Hellcats holding off more than 20 Zero-sens. In the fight that followed Clark managed to shoot down a 'Zeke' for his second kill of the day, but both his Hellcat and that of Ens Berube were badly shot up in the process. Having fought a large group of tenacious Zero-sens for 15 minutes, they finally escaped into cloud. However, Berube's F6F was so badly damaged that he eventually ditched and was never recovered.

By coincidence Lt(jg)s Hugh Batten and Samuel Brocato of VF-83 both became aces on the same mission on this day. They had each claimed two 'Jacks' apiece on 19 March, Brocato's victory coming ten days after he joined VF-83 – his first combat squadron. Later in the afternoon Batten and Brocato were sent aloft on a special CAP, with Batten leading the section. A little after 1715 hrs, they were flying near the island of Yoronjima when they came across a formation of nine 'Zekes' carrying bombs that were most likely from one of the IJN's kamikaze units. The aircraft were flying under an 8/10ths cloud layer in a thick haze. Using the cloud and haze to their advantage, the two pilots managed to attack undetected. In quick and carefully coordinated runs, Batten and Brocato shot down four Zero-sens each. For their skill in downing eight of the nine fighters, both men received the Navy Cross.

In VF-30's squadron history 6 April was recorded as 'Turkey Shoot Number Two'. Fourteen Hellcat pilots were flying a CAP north of Okinawa when they began to run into small formations of Japanese aircraft – usually three to four aeroplanes in loose formation. After landing, one pilot said 'It was like an Easter egg hunt – look under any cloud and there would be a Jap plane or two'. In a continuous series of running battles over the next two hours VF-30 pilots claimed 47 Japanese aircraft shot down (26 'Vals',14 'Zekes', five 'Tojos' and two 'Oscars'). The Hellcat pilots found the Japanese pilots to be very inexperienced, failing to take any evasive action except to dodge into a nearby cloud, and failing to offer mutual protection.

Towards the end of the patrol VF-30 came across a formation of 20 aircraft (that were identified as 'Vals') coming in low over the water with no fighter escort. Each aeroplane was carrying a large bomb and had no rear gunner. The pilots again seemed to be inexperienced, never using evasive action – probably a confirmation that they were indeed from one of the Special Attack units, having received little training. As the Aircraft Action report said, 'these aircraft were gleefully assaulted by the fighters, and to their knowledge only one of them made it through to attack naval vessels'.

It was a day for the ensigns, as three of them from VF-30 became 'aces in a day'. In the lead was Ens

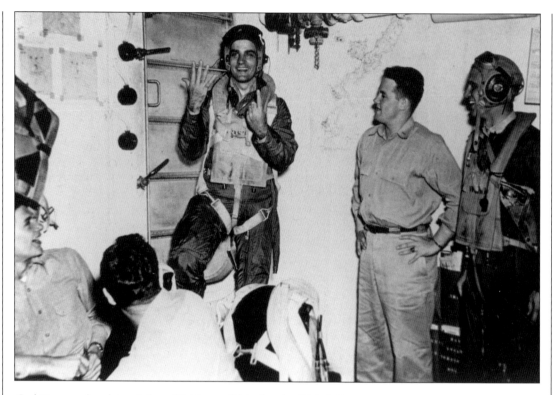

Carl Foster, who claimed three 'Vals', two 'Tojos' and a 'Zeke'. Ens Kenneth Dahms was given credit for 5.5 aircraft, namely three 'Vals', two 'Zekes' and a half-share in an 'Oscar', while Ens Johnnie Miller also claimed three 'Vals', a 'Tojo' and a 'Zeke'. Four other ensigns, Michele Mazzocco, Austin Olsen, David Philips and James Reber, were credited with four victories each. These kills were Reber's last, taking his total to 11. Lt(jg) Harvey Sturdevant got a 'Zeke' and two 'Vals' to make ace.

The presence of 'Tojos' and 'Oscars' in VF-30's claims raises the possibility that the Hellcat pilots had not always encountered 'Vals' during the afternoon combats, but JAAF 'Sonias' or 'Nates'.

VF-17 and its partner unit VBF-17 did well on this day too, the two squadrons claiming 46 aircraft during five CAPs. The main action came late in the afternoon when they ran into a large number of Japanese conventional and kamikaze aircraft attacking picket destroyers. When the fighting was over, the pilots submitted claims for 32 aircraft destroyed and six damaged.

Two divisions from VF-17 and two from VBF-17, under the leadership of VF-17's Lt Richard Cowger, had taken off from *Hornet* at 1538 hrs. Nearing their patrol area, Cowger was ordered to fly ten miles north of the island of Ie Shima to intercept a large incoming raid and protect the nearby picket destroyers. As they approached their CAP station the pilots could see streams of Japanese aeroplanes coming towards them in ones and twos (mostly 'Vals' and 'Zekes') carrying bombs and heading for the American ships. Cowger quickly flamed a 'Val' – the first of three. In an attempt to cope more effectively with the sheer number of enemy aeroplanes approaching them, Cowger ordered his divisions to split up into sections.

Ens Carl Foster, shown here holding up six fingers for his victories on 6 April, was VF-30's high scorer for the day (*John Lambert Collection, Museum of Flight*)

Ens Foster claimed just one 'Zeke' in his 6 April haul, and that aircraft was captured on film by his gun camera seconds prior to its demise. Foster was also credited with 1.5 'Zekes' six days later (*American Fighter Aces Association, Museum of Flight*)

Leading a section of VBF-17 Hellcats, Ensign Harold Yeremian downed two 'Zekes' and a 'Val' to make ace, while his wingman, Ens William Kostik, claimed two 'Vals, a 'Zeke' and a 'Myrt' for his first kills of the war. Yeremian's division leader led the formation to intercept five 'Vals', the leader and his wingman getting one. Kostick then led Ens Yeremian towards four more 'Vals', which they attacked. The Aircraft Action Report gives an idea of the intensity of the combat;

'One "Val" was flying alone. Kostik made a tail-on approach, opened fire into his wing roots and the "Val" crashed in flames. Ens Kostick observed the last aeroplane of the original five split to the right and head away from the fight. He tailed in on him and fired. The "Val" started smoking and spiralled into the water. The division had joined up and was returning to Point Nan when the call came advising us that the two destroyers bearing 030 from the orbit point were being attacked.

'Course was set for the DDs, and approaching their position, Ens Yeremian "tallyhoed" five or six "bogies" between the division and the DDs. Yeremian attacked a "Zeke", which started to climb to escape. He opened fire from below and the "Zeke" started burning from the wing roots and fell into the water. A second "Zeke" of the group was brought under fire by Yeremian. It took violent evasive action. However, the VBF-17 pilot was able to spray rounds all over him from close range astern. The "Zeke" went into a steep dive and didn't pull out. Kostik took a third "Zeke", which was low on the water. He made a highside approach on him. The "Zeke" smoked and hit the water.

'The next aeroplane sighted by this group was a "Myrt". Ens Kostik saw him heading straight for one of the destroyers, with a bomb under his belly. He fired a long burst over his nose. The "Myrt" turned away from the DD and started to climb. Kostik closed on him to a range of 200 ft astern and opened fire. Only one gun fired – tracers hit the port wing of the Jap. Kostik fired again, this time with three guns working, into the engine and the cockpit. The "Myrt" dropped one wing, hit the water and exploded. Near the end of the fight Ens Yeremian added one more "Val" to his score. This one was flying 20 ft off the water. Yeremian made a full deflection attack on his beam. The "Val" started smoking and went down.'

High scorer for the mission was VF-17's Lt(jg) Willis Hardy, who became an 'ace in a day'. Hardy and his wingman, Lt(jg) Harrison Morgan, downed eight aircraft between them, Hardy getting his last kill (a 'Judy') just as the sun was setting. Years later he recalled that the prospect of making a night carrier landing, which he had never done before, was far more worrying to him than combat with enemy aircraft.

Several pilots who later became aces scored victories during the day's actions. Four divisions of VF-45 on CAP over Okinawa were directed to split up to provide cover for radar picket destroyers off the coast in the face of the on-coming Japanese raid. In the running combats that followed the squadron claimed 24 aircraft destroyed. Lt James Cain, leading one of the divisions, claimed a 'Hamp', a 'Val' and a 'Zeke', as well as a half-share in a second 'Zeke', Lt(jg) Robert Woolverton got two 'Vals' and a half-share in a 'Zeke', and Lt(jg) Harry Swinburne two 'Zekes'.

In VF-82, which was also caught up in the late afternoon battles covering the picket destroyers, Lt Robert Jennings shot down three

'Zekes' and 'Vals' were the most commonly encountered Japanese aircraft, and they suffered accordingly. A 'Val' stood little chance against a Hellcat or Corsair, and this particular example fell to a VF-45 pilot on 6 April (*NARA VF-45 Aircraft Action Report for 6 April 1945*)

'Vals' – one well within the range of a destroyer's fire. Lt(jg) Clarence Davies accounted for an 'Oscar', two 'Vals' and a half-share in a third dive-bomber.

The squadron Aircraft Action Report commented that 'Of all the enemy planes encountered, *not one returned fire* – all remained on course, boring in towards the surface vessels. The only evasive action offered was jinking, and the majority of the aircraft were obsolete models as can be seen by the list of types destroyed. Primary danger to our pilots was collision, or getting in the path of a friendly aeroplane's fire'.

The next day, 7 April, saw the super battleship *Yamato* make its failed kamikaze sortie to Okinawa. Many of the carrier fighter squadrons were involved in supporting the dive- and torpedo-bombers in their attacks on *Yamato* and its escorts. A much reduced Special Attack effort saw just nine Zero-sen kamikaze from the 721st Kokutai, 25 Zero-sens from the 252nd Kokutai, nine 'Frances' from the 706th and 762nd Kokutai and 11 'Judys' from the 601st Kokutai, with an escort of 78 Zero-sens, set out shortly before noon to attack carriers reported to the east of Okinawa.

Returning from a mission to monitor the advancing *Yamato* in the early afternoon, Lt(jg) Lindley Godson of VBF-83 came across two 'Judys' approaching the task force, which was just 15 miles away. Godson and his wingman gave chase and quickly shot both down.

Lt(jg) Byron Eberts of VBF-17 downed a 'Frances' in the afternoon for his fifth kill, while Lt(jg) Harris Mitchell of VF-9 also claimed a 'Frances' for his first victory.

Earlier in the day Lt James Cain of VF-45 claimed a 'Val' for his fifth and final victory of the war, while his squadronmate Lt(jg) Norman Mollard claimed a 'Nick' in the afternoon for his first victory.

Lt Armand Manson of VF-82 was leading a section in a division CAP that ran into a small formation of fighters identified as a 'George' and several 'Franks'. He attacked the 'George', which exploded when his fire hit the engine. Manson and his wingman then spotted two 'Franks', which they promptly despatched.

Although wildly over-estimating the number of American ships sunk or damaged, Combined Fleet headquarters judged Kikusui Operation No 1 to have been a success. Based on reconnaissance reports, the Japanese believed the Special Attack forces had sunk two battleships, two

An F6F-5 of VF-82 has its engine run up to full power on the deck of *Bennington* moments before being launched on a mission during April 1945 (*NARA 80G-314588*)

carriers, three cruisers, eight destroyers and five transports, with many more ships damaged. Success was attributed to the strategy of massed, simultaneous attacks, and the fact that the airfields on Okinawa were not yet capable of supporting American air units. However, the Japanese lacked the personnel and aircraft to quickly mount another mass attack. Smaller Special Attack missions would be flown almost daily, but it would take another five days before a sufficient number of Special Attack units could be organised for the next Kikusui operation.

For the US Navy units off Okinawa, 6 April would prove to be the worst day of the Okinawa campaign. It was impossible for the CAPs to stop every kamikaze, and inevitably some made it through to the fleet. While the ships' AAA shot down many aircraft, 20 ships were hit on this day and six were sunk, including two destroyers on radar picket duty. The radar pickets would bear the brunt of the kamikaze attacks during the Okinawa campaign. On 7 April a kamikaze hit *Hancock*, dropping a bomb on the port catapult and cartwheeling across the deck into the aircraft parked aft. The crew managed to get the fires out and resume operations, at a cost of 62 dead and 71 wounded, but the carrier had to be sent back to Pearl Harbor for repairs.

KIKUSUI NO 2 – 12-13 APRIL 1945

Both sides now prepared for the next onslaught. As part of these preparations, two Marine Air Groups arrived on Okinawa for the Tactical Air Force. On 7 April Marine Air Group (MAG) 31 began operations from Yontan with three Corsair squadrons and one night fighter unit (VMF-224, 311 and 441 and VMF(N)-542). MAG-33 arrived at Kadena airfield on 9 April, bringing in the same complement (VMF-312, 322 and 323 and VMF(N)-543). More Marine Corps and USAAF fighter squadrons would arrive over the next two months to take over responsibility for the air defence of Okinawa from TF 58. The faster Marine Corps Corsairs were desperately needed to help defend against the kamikaze attacks, leaving the more numerous, and slower US Navy F6Fs to provide close air support to the divisions fighting on the ground.

The arrival of the Corsairs was timely, as the Japanese launched Kikusui Operation No 2 on 12 April. This was the second-largest mass kamikaze attack of the war, with 125 IJN and 60 JAAF kamikaze

aeroplanes taking part. Commencing around noon, 34 'George' fighters from the 343rd Kokutai and 15 JAAF fighters were sent aloft to maintain air superiority over the Kikaiga Shima and Amami Oshima island groups and along the route the kamikaze would take. To secure air superiority over Okinawa, 72 Zero-sens took off in three waves. The IJN's kamikaze aircraft that day included 29 'Vals', some 16 of which were from the Hachiman Goko-u-tai (which also sent out ten 'Kates'), six 'Kates' from the Jobanchuku-tai and 17 older A6M2 Zero-sens from the Motoyama-Ku. Later in the afternoon the JAAF sortied 60 Special Attack aircraft, nearly half of which were obsolete 'Nates' and 'Sonias' from the 69th, 75th, 102nd, 103rd and 104th Tokubetsu-tai.

Among of the first American units to encounter the attack were three divisions from VF-82 that were flying a CAP near Amami Oshima. At 1230 hrs the patrol saw Japanese fighters heading north, identifying them as two 'Tojos' and a 'Jack'. Lt Armand Manson downed a 'Tojo' and shared the 'Jack' with his wingman. These victories made Manson an ace. A short time later three divisions from VBF-17, led by Lt Edwin Conant, ran into the 343rd Kokutai's fighter sweep. After being relieved from their CAP over Kiki Shima, two divisions began a strafing attack on Wan airfield on the island, with the third remaining above for cover.

Lt Naoshi Kanno, leading the formation of Shiden-Kai, saw the Hellcats strafing below him and attacked VBF-17's third division, shooting down Ens Raymond Grosso. Hearing the warnings of attacking Japanese aircraft, Conant led his division up and into the fight. Firing a snap shot at what he identified as a 'Zeke', he knocked pieces off its wing and tail. Catching a second Japanese aircraft, which Conant again misidentified as a 'Zeke', on the tail of a Hellcat, he closed to within 300 ft and fired. Setting the 'George' ablaze, Conant watched it spin down into the sea. Spotting another 'George' ahead of him, which he claimed was a 'Tojo', Conant closed to within 75 ft before opening fire. Seeing hits on the tail, fuselage and wings, his burst may have also killed the pilot, as the 'George' did a slow roll and then dove straight into the water. These two kills made Conant an ace.

Lt Cdr Marshal Beebe was leading three divisions of sister-squadron VF-17 on a CAP in the area when he heard reports of the fighting over the radio. He immediately headed southwest towards the action. Closing

Marine Corps squadrons began to arrive at Yontan airfield, on Okinawa, on 7 April. Two days later MAG-33 commenced operations from Kadena. Here, one of the first Corsairs to arrive at the airfield, from VMF-312, taxis in (*US Marine Corps History Division (USMCHD)*)

in on the melee, Beebe spotted a Japanese fighter pulling out of the fight. Misidentifying this as a 'Jack', Beebe and his division got into a running fight with the 'George', which took violent evasive action but to no avail, as Beebe was finally able to close and shoot it down. Returning to the fight, Lt(jg) Frank Sistrunk made a head-on pass at a 'Zeke' and followed the fighter down in a split-S. As the 'Zeke' started to climb out, Sistrunk pulled up behind the fighter and set it on fire, the pilot bailing out. This was Sistrunk's third kill, and four days later he would become an ace.

Two other VF-17 pilots became aces that day. Lt(jg) Tillman Pool, leading a section in Lt Thomas Harris' division, was trying to catch up with the other VF-17 divisions heading towards the action when he saw four 'Franks' flying 3000 ft above him. He pulled up underneath one of them and fired, the 'Frank' bursting into flames and crashing into the sea below. Later in the afternoon Pool was flying with Lt(jg) Richard Cowger's division when they spotted four 'Zekes' flying south of them. Diving down on the IJN fighters, Pool attacked the last of the four, the 'Zeke' rolling over, bursting into flames and crashing. These two kills made Pool an ace. In this action Cowger also shot down one of the 'Zekes', getting a second one a little later for his fourth and fifth kills.

Lt(jg) Harris scored his last two kills of the war on this mission, flaming a 'George' in the fight with the 343rd Kokutai and then coming across one of the 'Kates' sent out on a kamikaze mission, which he promptly despatched. With additional kills from later patrols, VF-17 and VBF-17 claimed 32 Japanese aircraft shot down for the day.

With many Japanese conventional and kamikaze aircraft now streaming south, the combats continued throughout the afternoon. More US Navy and Marine Corps fighter squadrons were drawn into the fight including VF-30, whose ensigns added to their scores. Ens Michele Mazzocco claiming a 'Tojo' for his fifth kill, while Ens Carl Foster got 1.5 'Zekes' for his last kills of the war, taking his total to eight victories.

Two pilots from VF-83 became aces on this day. Lt(jg) Robert Hamilton was part of a division on a CAP flying at 20,000 ft over Okinawa when a "swarm" of Japanese aeroplanes appeared at the same altitude – a formation of single-engined bombers (which may have been the group of 'Kate' kamikaze aircraft) with an escort of Zero-sen fighters. Lt David Robinson, the division leader, ordered his pilots to circle around the large formation and attack the fighter escort from the rear. Hamilton and his wingman, Ens William Kingston, each flamed a 'Zeke' in their first pass. Pulling up, they saw a 'Tojo' ahead of them. As Hamilton opened fire on the fighter, a Zero-sen bounced his Hellcat. Kingston managed to get in a long burst at the latter machine as it climbed away, leaving it smoking. Seeing no other enemy fighters around, the two pilots followed the smoking Zero-sen and 'Tojo' down and saw them crash.

Marine Corps pilots from both carrier-based and land-based squadrons were active. 2Lt Dean Caswell was part of a division from VMF-221 that was escorting a photographic mission when reports of action came over the radio. Speeding toward the area, the division saw three aircraft they identified as 'Zekes' flying below them. Diving down, Caswell came in behind a 'Zeke', opened fire from the 'six o'clock' position and watched it crash onto Wan airfield. Caswell's wingman,

1Lt John McManus, got onto the tail of a fighter that he identified as a 'Frank', which was in turn being chased by three Corsairs. The latter machines broke off their attack when they ran into heavy AAA coming up from Wan airfield, but McManus continued to fire as the Japanese fighter led him across the field at an altitude of just 100 ft. He got in several good bursts before being driven off by the AAA. Caswell saw the Japanese fighter do a wingover and crash into the ground. VMF-221 pilots reported that what they identified as 'Zekes' and 'Franks' took 'amazing quantities of lead without burning', suggesting that the aircraft may have in fact been 'Georges' from the 343rd Kokutai.

Maj Archie Donahue, Executive Officer of VMF-451 aboard *Bunker Hill*, was an experienced fighter pilot with a record of nine victories flying F4F Wildcats and F4U Corsairs with VMF-112 in the Solomons campaign – his last victory had been over two 'Zekes' on 7 June 1943. Returning to combat with VMF-451, Donahue had been scoreless up to this point in his second combat tour. He was leading one of three divisions of VMF-451 on a CAP west of Okinawa during the afternoon of 12 April when they ran into a large formation of Japanese aeroplanes – 20+ 'Vals', all carrying bombs, several 'Kates' and an escort of ten 'Zekes'. Donahue quickly assumed the lead of the three divisions and coordinated the attacks, which resulted in claims for 16 aeroplanes shot down, including ten of the 'Vals', five 'Zekes' and a single 'Kate'. Donahue personally claimed three 'Vals' and two 'Zekes', and was awarded the Navy Cross for his exceptional leadership.

It had been a day of intensive combat, almost all the fighting taking place in the afternoon. By dusk on the 12th US Navy pilots had claimed 144 Japanese aeroplanes shot down and their Marine Corps compatriots a further 77. But a number of kamikaze had managed to break through the CAPs to attack American ships, hitting 18 and sinking one LCS(L). Again, the destroyers and destroyer escorts took the brunt of the attack.

Maj Archie Donahue, who became an ace in the Southwest Pacific flying Wildcats and Corsairs with VMF-112, was executive officer of VMF-451 aboard *Bunker Hill* when he claimed six victories on 12 April (*USMCHD*)

KIKUSUI NO 3 – 15-16 APRIL 1945

The Japanese had again suffered heavy losses during Kikusui No 2, IJN and JAAF fighters having been unable to establish air superiority along the route taken by the Special Attack aircraft to the American fleet. While preparing for the next mass attack, on 14 April the IJN sent out a smaller force of kamikaze, consisting of older A6M2 Zero-sens from the Da-roku Kenbutai, Dai-ni Chikubutai, Dai-ni Shinkentai and the Dai-ichi Showatai, and seven 'Betty' bombers from the 721st Kokutai carrying Ohka piloted rocket bombs. A large escort of 125 Zero-sen and Shiden-Kai fighters accompanied the Special Attack aeroplanes.

Flying on separate missions VF-17 and VBF-17 both ran into this Japanese force. VF-17 had sent off five divisions on a combined photo-reconnaissance escort and strike mission on an island airfield south of Kyushu. Atround 1300 hrs Lt(jg) Billy Watts was escorting the photo aeroplanes with his division west of Kikaiga Shima when he spotted a 'Betty' bomber carrying an Ohka beneath its fuselage flying at 11,000 ft – this was one of the aircraft from the 721st Kokutai. Diving down, Watts opened fire in a high-side run from the 'four o'clock' position, getting hits on the starboard engine, which burst into flamea. The 'Betty' jettisoned the Ohka, which crashed into the sea below. On Watts' third run the 'Betty's' starboard wing collapsed and the aeroplane spiralled into the sea. A short time later Watts' section leader found another 721st Kokutai 'Betty' and shot it down too.

An hour later four divisions from VBF-17 were on a CAP 30 miles from the Task Force. Lt(jg) John Johnston was leading his division at 7000 ft when he received word of bogeys approaching, and was vectored out to intercept. The division found eight 'Zekes' ahead of them, flying about 1500 ft below, and two 'Zekes' at the same level. Coming in behind one of the 'Zeke' section leaders, Johnston began firing at 900 ft and closed to within 25 ft, getting hits on the wing root and setting the cockpit on fire. He next attacked the formation leader, pulling into a 'six o'clock' position and firing until he was almost on top of the 'Zeke', which burst into flames and crashed into the sea. Johnston shot down his third 'Zeke' moments later, this aircraft having been on the tail of a Hellcat. Ens Robert Clark claimed two 'Zekes' for his fourth and fifth kills, Ens William Kostik got one for his fifth, and last, kill of the war, and Ens Byron Eberts, flying with another division, claimed a 'Kate' for his fifth, and final, victory.

The next day the IJN and JAAF suspended daylight special attacks in order to prepare for Kikusui No 3. TF 58 chose this day to send fighter sweeps over the airfields on Kyushu, TG 58.1 sending out a strong force of fighters from VF-17, VBF-17, VF-30 and VF-82 to attack Kanoya airfield. Lt Robert Jennings led seven aircraft from VF-82 in the attack, bombing and strafing the base. Coming out of a run, Jennings found a 'Jack' ahead of him and got in several good bursts, but the fighter did not crash. Retiring to the east, the division saw three 'Jacks' over Shibushi Bay. Jennings shot one of them down for his fifth kill and damaged a second. Lt Omer Donahue attacked the third 'Jack', setting it on fire. He then pulled up alongside the burning fighter, whereupon the IJN pilot rolled back his canopy, motioned at Donahue to move away and bailed out.

15 April also saw TG 58.3 send a force of eight Hellcats and eight Corsairs from VF-83 and VBF-83, together with Hellcats from VF-47 off USS *Bataan* (CVL-29) and Corsairs from VF-84 off *Bunker Hill*, to strike Kanoya East airfield with 500-lb bombs and high-velocity aerial rockets (HVARs). Lt Thomas Reidy, acting CO of VBF-83, was getting his two divisions back together after their strafing runs on the field when six to ten single-engined fighters attacked them. Lt Reidy shot down what he claimed was an 'Oscar' on his first pass through the attacking aircraft, then got onto the tail of a second Ki-43 and set it on fire for his fifth and sixth kills. These may have actually been Zero-sen fighters from the 203rd Kokutai, which had taken off to defend their airfield.

Four pilots from VF-82 became aces during the Okinawa campaign. Lt Robert Jennings scored his first victories flying F4Fs with VF-72. He claimed a 'Tojo' during the February 1945 strikes on Tokyo, and six kills during the Okinawa campaign to become VF-82's leading ace (*American Fighter Aces Association, Museum of Flight*)

Lt Thomas Reidy, who was a former SB2C Helldiver pilot, served as acting CO of VBF-83 during April 1945. A successful fighter pilot, he scored his first two victories on 18 March. On 15 April Reidy claimed two 'Oscars' to become an ace (*NARA 80G-348145*)

Kikusui No 3 began shortly after dawn on 16 April. At around 0630 hrs 32 Shiden-Kai fighters from the 343rd Kokutai took off on an air superiority mission to clear the skies of American aircraft around Kikaiga Shima and Amami Oshima for the kamikaze aircraft that were to follow. These began taking off in separate waves composed of Zero-sen escorts, Special Attack aeroplanes and conventional carrier and twin-engined bombers. The Special Attack aircraft were a collection of older Zero-sen fighters, 'Kates', 'Vals' and more modern 'Myrts' and 'Frances'. Many different units contributed kamikaze aircraft, including the 701st, 721st and 732nd Kokutai. Two waves of 76 Zero-sens, 50 Special Attack aeroplanes, ten 'Judys' and eight 'Frances' bombers headed for the American carriers, while a further 52 Zero-sens escorted ten 'Kate', 19 'Val', 12 'Frances' and ten 'Myrt' Special Attack aircraft, with still more Zero-sen Special Attack aeroplanes, towards Okinawa.

The JAAF sent off 45 kamikaze aircraft on this day too, consisting of 45 obsolete 'Nate' fighters from the 40th, 79th, 106th, 107th and 109th Tokubetsu-tai. US Navy and Marine Corps fighter squadrons were up in force to repel this mass attack, the former claiming 157 aircraft and the latter 46, making this the third-highest scoring day of the campaign. By dusk on 16 April 13 pilots had achieved their fifth victories.

Realistically, the 343rd Kokutai had little chance of winning air superiority against superior numbers of American Hellcats and Corsairs. Flying to the north of Amami Oshima, the 343rd's 1st Chutai was attempting a bounce on 12 Hellcats from VF-47 when two of VF-17's divisions attacked the Chutai unseen from below and behind as it was circling to attack the Hellcats. Lt(jg) Charles 'Billy' Watts quickly took over the two VF-17 divisions when Lt Jim Pearce's guns failed to fire. As Watts recalled years later, 'I know they didn't see us until we were in on them and firing. We came in there and they didn't move or anything. After about seven or eight minutes our part was over because we'd burned out our guns. We'd shot down a total of seven, and none of us got hit'.

Watts first attacked a 'George' from behind, which he later identified as a 'Frank', opening fire at 800 ft and closing to 200 ft, at which point the IJN fighter started smoking, rolled over to the right and spiralled down into the sea. Watts then found another 'George' making a turn to the right, and he quickly came in behind it and opened fire at 1200 ft. Closing to 300 ft, he saw hits in the cockpit area and the engine. Again the 'George' started smoking and, like Watts' first victim, rolled over onto its back and crashed into the sea. These were Watts' fifth and sixth kills, making him an ace.

It would be a long day for Watts. Returning to *Hornet*, he and three other pilots were told to land on *Bennington* as their carrier was launching aircraft. Once aboard, the pilots had a cup of coffee while their Hellcats were refuelled and the machine guns replaced and re-armed. They then took off on their second CAP, during which Watts shot down a 'Francis' for his seventh, and final, kill of the war. Returning from the CAP, the pilots were told to land on *Belleau Wood*, where they grabbed a sandwich before taking off on their third CAP of the day. The division eventually returned to *Hornet* at dusk, having spent more than ten hours in the air.

While the fighter battles were raging over the islands, other squadrons were sweeping the airfields of southern Kyushu. Three divisions from

F4U-1D Corsairs aboard *Bunker Hill*. VF-84 and the two Marine Corps (VMF-221 and VMF-451) Corsair squadrons assigned to the vessel used these fighters interchangeably (*NARA 80G-315236*)

VBF-17 and one from VF-17 joined a group from VF-84 in an attack on Kanoya airfield. As the group was over Kagoshima Bay, a group of 21 'Zekes' – one formation of nine aeroplanes at 11,000 ft and anothr of 12 at 9000 ft – was spotted over the JAAF airfield at Chiran to the west. Lt(jg) John Johnston of VBF-17, who had shot down three 'Zekes' two days earlier, now went one better. VBF-17's Aircraft Action Report described the combat in detail;

'Lt(jg) Johnston's division, at 13,000 ft, started for the top group of "bogies". The nine "Zekes" were flying a loose formation all at the same altitude, with a "V" of three aeroplanes leading, followed by a four-aeroplane division behind and to the starboard of the leading "V" and a two-aeroplane section bringing up the rear. Johnston nosed down and led his division towards the formation from astern. He chose the last aeroplane in the group, pulled up on its tail to a range of 600 ft and opened fire at the cockpit. The aeroplane started burning in that area and went down flaming all over. Johnston then "hurdled" the next two aeroplanes and hit the section leader of the four-aeroplane division. He shot him down in an attack similar to the first, the aeroplane crashing in flames. He then skipped another aeroplane and hit the division leader, opening fire at "six o'clock". The "Zeke's" port wing fell away and the aeroplane disintegrated in mid-air. Lt Johnston's last aeroplane was the leader of the formation. It was also attacked from "six o'clock" at close range. The "Zeke" caught fire, pieces started falling off and it crashed.'

Johnston claimed an additional two 'Zekes' as damaged. Over the space of four days he had shot down eight Japanese aircraft.

As the waves of kamikaze proceeded south they ran into US Navy and Marine Corps squadrons on CAP north of Okinawa over the radar picket destroyers. Lt(jg) Philip Kirkwood of VF-10, flying off *Intrepid*, was leading a division, with Ens Norwald Quiel as his wingman, and Ens Horace Heath leading the second section, with Ens Alfred Lerch as his

wingman. The division was orbiting over a radar picket ship at 10,000 ft when they were vectored onto IJN 'Vals' and JAAF 'Nates' flying south in two small formations. Kirkwood split the division, diving down below a layer of cloud with Heath, whose radio was not working, while Quiel and Lerch went above.

When Lerch called out a formation of two 'Vals' and one 'Nate' the division made a high-speed climb and came in from behind, shooting down all three aeroplanes – Quiel got the 'Nate' and Kirkwood and Lerch a 'Val' apiece. Heath found another 'Val' ducking into the clouds, and shot it down. The division then became separated, but Kirkwood and Quiel joined up and returned to the radar picket ship, only to find that it had already been hit by a kamikaze. They were soon vectored onto another formation of 'Vals' and 'Nates' that were targeting another radar picket destroyer some 20 miles away. Intercepting the formation, Kirkwood downed a 'Val' and a 'Nate', while Quiel claimed two 'Nates'.

The two pilots covered the destroyer for the next hour, Kirkwood shooting down two more 'Nates' and Quiel getting a third. The pilots often dived through the destroyer's AAA to catch the aircraft before they could hit the ship.

Returning to the rendezvous point, they saw AAA from other picket ships just as a 'Nate' was about to begin its final dive. Kirkwood managed to catch up with the JAAF fighter just over the water, and he shot it down for his sixth kill of the day.

Heath and Lerch were in a battle of their own, having joined up after the first attack. They ran into a large formation of 'Nates' north of Okinawa, these fighters almost certainly being some of the 45 kamikaze aircraft that set off from Kyushu earlier that morning. The 'Nates' were flying in three-aeroplane sections, and each carried one or two bombs. The two pilots attacked the formation, each shooting down a 'Nate'. This attack broke up the JAAF formation, which proceeded to mill

VF-10, which flew F4U-1Ds off *Intrepid*, had its best day on 16 April during the second Kikusui operation when its pilots claimed 32 aircraft shot down (*NARA 80G-316035*)

Lt(jg) Philip Kirkwood's division claimed 20 of VF-10's victories on 16 April. Kirkwood was credited with six of them to become an 'ace in a day', while Ens Alfred Lerch, in the division's other section, claimed seven (*American Fighter Aces Association, Museum of Flight*)

around above the sea as if not knowing quite what to do. This allowed Lerch to rapidly shoot down three more aeroplanes, and then chase another three towards Okinawa. Heath arrived to shoot down one from this formation, with Lerch getting another. The two pilots then chased another 'Nate', Lerch shooting this one down for his seventh kill.

In total, Kirkwood's division claimed 20 aircraft for the day. Kirkwood and Lerch each received the Navy Cross and Quiel a Silver Star for their actions. This would be the last combat for VF-10, as a kamikaze hit *Intrepid* during the day, forcing its withdrawal for repairs.

On 16 April VF-17's Lt(jg) Ted Crosby was flying as wingman to Lt Millard 'Fuzz' Wooley, who was in turn leading his division in an orbit at 8000 ft over a radar picket destroyer northeast of Okinawa. Arriving on station the vessel's fighter director said, 'Keep in mind, gentlemen, we are the third destroyer out here. The other two have been sunk'. A short while later Wooley received a vector onto a group of approaching Japanese aeroplanes and initiated a high-speed climb to 25,000 ft. Crosby was having trouble with his supercharger control and finally had to place his knee against the lever to hold it in high blower.

Reaching altitude, the division saw a formation of 12 aircraft that they identified as 'Jacks' and 'Zekes' at 25,000 ft, with another group of eight 2000 ft below them. These fighters were most likely the escort for a group of kamikaze. Wooley, an aggressive pilot, charged right into the larger formation, and in three passes he shot down two of the 'Jacks' and damaged a third. Crosby dove on the lower formation, also shooting down two of the 'Jacks', before climbing back up to join Wooley. Crosby shot down a 'Jack' and a 'Zeke' in successive passes. Returning to the rendezvous point, the division ran into a number of 'Vals' attacking the picket ships. Wooley shot down a 'Val' and, with Crosby and another member of the division, chased a second machine and overran it. Climbing steeply up into a split-S, Crosby dove vertically on the 'Val', hitting its engine and sending the dive-bomber crashing into the sea. He had just become VF-17's fourth 'ace in a day' for the Okinawa campaign.

Flying in one of three divisions from VF-45 off USS *San Jacinto* (CVL-30), Lt(jg) Norman Mollard Jr had his own unique adventure. Following his division leader in an attack on a small formation of 'Zekes', Mollard dove after another 'Zeke' a few miles away and slightly above in

VF-17 produced four 'aces in a day' during the Okinawa campaign. Lt(jg) John 'Ted' Crosby was the last pilot from the unit to achieve this distinction, claiming four fighters and a 'Val' on 16 April for his only victories of the war (*American Fighter Aces Association, Museum of Flight*)

An F6F-5 of VF-45 waits to take off from *San Jacinto*. VF-45 scored well during the Kikusui attacks on 6 April, claiming 23 aircraft shot down. Ten days later the unit claimed an additional 14 victories (*NARA 80G-314829*)

Lt(jg) Norman Mollard of VF-45 did well on 16 April, claiming four victories on his own and being awarded the Navy Cross (*NARA 80G-265732*)

VMF-441 was one of the Marine Corps Corsair squadrons that did well on 16 April, claiming 15.5 aeroplanes shot down. The successful pilots stand in front of Capt Floyd Kirkpatrick's Corsair, *Palpitatin' Pauli*, named after his wife. Kirkpatrick, kneeling on the left, shot down three 'Vals' and 2Lt Selva McGinty, standing on the right, claimed two 'Vals' and a fighter. Kirkpatrick and McGinty were the squadron's only aces of the campaign (*NARA 208-AA-PAC-Box 87-Folder A-3-10046*)

a gentle glide. Coming in unseen below the fighter, Mollard opened fire from 500 ft, getting good hits on the fuselage and wing. The 'Zeke' erupted in flames, then blew up. Mollard turned back to link up with his division when he saw a Corsair pursuing a 'Val', calling out to anyone that he had a 'Zeke' on his tail. Mollard dove toward the fighter, which broke away and came at him in a head-on pass instead. Pulling straight up, Mollard saw the 'Zeke' pilot attempt to follow him, but stall out and go into a dive. Mollard did a wing over and came down after the 'Zeke', closing the range as the IJN pilot pulled out of his dive. Raking the fuselage and probably killing the pilot, Mollard watched as the 'Zeke' spun down into the sea below.

He then rejoined the Corsair pilot who was still chasing the 'Val', although the F4U appeared to be out of ammunition. Mollard pulled ahead and fired a long burst into the dive-bomber, which started smoking. He chopped his throttle, came in on the tail of the 'Val' and fired another burst. It burst into flames and crashed into the sea. Heading back towards his division, Mollard saw another 'Val' flying above several minesweepers. Diving down, he came in on the tail of the aircraft, chopped his throttle and began firing with the only gun that remained serviceable. The 'Val' turned towards a minesweeper as Mollard continued to fire, seeing his bursts hitting the its wings and fuselage. Soon the aeroplane was enveloped in flames, and it crashed just short of the minesweeper. The day's action brought Mollard's tally to six victories, earning him the Navy Cross.

VMF-441, flying a CAP to the west of Okinawa, ran into a large formation of 25 aircraft identified as 'Bettys', 'Vals' and 'Zekes'. Three divisions of Corsairs went after the formation, and in a matter of minutes they had claimed 15.5 aeroplanes shot down. Capt Floyd Kirkpatrick, leading one of the divisions, claimed three 'Vals', while 2Lt Selva McGinty, a wingman in the second division, claimed two 'Vals' and a single 'Zeke'. The Aircraft Action Report noted that the Japanese pilots did not employ any evasive action apart from gentle turns.

In one of those curious twists of luck that occurred during this campaign against the kamikaze, 2Lt William Eldridge Jr accounted for two 'Vals', a 'Zeke' and a 'Betty' (likely an Ohka-carrying bomber from the 721st Kokutai), but apparently never encountered Japanese aircraft again during his tour, thus narrowly missing out on becoming an ace. A number of US Navy and Marine Corps pilots downed three or four aircraft in a single mission on their only encounter with the JAAF or IJN.

INTERREGNUM

Following the attack on 16 April, weather conditions and the depletion of Special Attack units within both the JAAF and IJN forced the postponement of the next Kikusui operation for 12 days. This gave the naval vessels off Okinawa a welcome reprieve. The kamikaze had damaged three fleet carriers – *Hancock*, *Enterprise* and *Intrepid* – sufficiently enough for them to have to be withdrawn.

Being targeted by a kamikaze was nerve-wracking, and the men on the ships that were performing radar picket duty suffered the most as they bore the brunt of the attacks. On board other vessels in the fleet, waiting for the outcome of a raid was never easy. As John Larkin, a pilot with VF-83, recalled, 'It was something to live under, when we were under a kamikaze attack, which was frequent. You always heard the five-inch guns, which were the big ones, going "boom, boom, boom". Then after that you'd hear the 40 mm start to go, then finally when they were really in close you'd hear the 20 mm go off. And at that point you just waited for what was going to happen next'.

Two air battles of note took place during this period, on 17 and 22 April. On the 17th, beginning at around 0700 hrs, the Fifth Air Fleet sent out 30 kamikaze aircraft with ten 'Judy' and four 'Frances' bombers and an escort of 62 Zero-sens – 34 Shiden-Kai fighters had preceded them to cover the route to the American carriers. That same day the JAAF's 62nd Sentai despatched at least eight 'Frank' fighters on a Special Attack mission, but it is unclear whether they accompanied the IJN formation. It is more likely that the 'Frank' pilots were on their own separate mission to Okinawa, given the division of responsibilities between the JAAF and IJN Special Attack units, with the latter concentrating on US Navy warships.

That morning Lt Eugene Valencia of VF-9, flying off *Yorktown*, was leading two divisions on a CAP north of TG 58.4 when he was vectored onto an approaching formation of Japanese aircraft. VF-9 had been flying missions since the attacks on Kyushu in March, but up to this point had engaged Japanese aircraft infrequently, the squadron claiming only 20 aircraft destroyed up to this date.

Heading north to meet the oncoming Japanese, Valencia sighted a group of 38 aircraft that he identified as 'Franks' and 'Zekes'. Given the carrier pilots' unfamiliarity with the 'George', and the repeated confusion in identifying the newer Japanese fighter as a 'Frank', it is highly likely that the formation Valencia was about to attack was comprised of the Shiden-Kai fighters sent out earlier that morning on the air superiority mission, and not the 'Franks' that also sortied that day. Adding some credence to this interpretation is the fact that at approximately the same time Hellcats from VF-12 ran into a small formation of 'Franks' south of Kikaiga Shima, claiming five shot down. Ironically, a sixth was claimed as a 'George'!

By this point in the war Valencia was a highly experienced Hellcat pilot with 10.5 victories to his name. In between his first and second combat tours

Lt Eugene Valencia became an ace during his first tour with VF-9 in 1943-44. During his second tour in 1945 he claimed an additional 15.5 aircraft to raise his wartime score to 23. He duly tied with Lt Cecil Harris as the US Navy's second-ranking ace (*NARA 80G-376283*)

with VF-9 he had trained the pilots of his division in air combat tactics, perfecting what he called the 'mowing machine', where one section would initiate an attack while the other section provided cover, then reverse the roles. This would be the first real opportunity to put his tactics into practice.

Climbing into the Japanese formation, Valencia and his wingman, Lt(jg) Harris Mitchell, came out of the sun to attack two fighters they identified as 'Franks'. Valencia shot one down, after which he ordered his other section (consisting of Lt James French and Lt(jg) Clinton Smith) to join his in the coordinated section attacks they were trained for. The enemy formation broke apart and entered a circle to the left, slowly losing altitude. Valencia kept his division high, making repeated attacks from above on enemy aeroplanes that tried to get on the tails of the other Hellcats. In a ten-minute fight Valencia claimed six 'Franks' shot down and two more damaged, French claimed four 'Zekes' destroyed, Mitchell three 'Zekes' destroyed and Smith one 'Frank' destroyed and another probably destroyed. Valencia was awarded the Navy Cross for his leadership and flying skill on this mission.

During the late afternoon of 22 April VMF-323 had one of the most successful combats of its tour. The Fifth Air Fleet had sent out a small number of kamikaze to attack the American carriers early in the morning. In the late afternoon the Sixth Air Army sent out its own Special Attack mission against shipping around Okinawa. The 80th and 81st Shinbutai sortied 22 'Sonias' and the 105th and 109th Shinbutai contributed 11 'Nates' (it is possible that other JAAF Shinbutai units participated that day too, but this formation seems to conform to what VMF-323 engaged).

Maj George Axtell, VMF-323's CO, was leading seven Corsairs on a CAP when, after three hours on patrol west of Okinawa near the island of Aguni Shima, they were told to intercept bogies coming in at low altitude over the sea. Diving through a layer of cloud, Axtell came out to see a formation of aircraft that he identified as approximately 35 'Vals' and 'Nates', all carrying bombs. Given the rough similarity in outline between the 'Val' and the 'Sonia', the fact that the pilots clearly identified 'Nates' as part of the formation, and the similarity in the number of aircraft involved, it seems highly likely that this was the group of kamikaze from the 80th, 81st, 105th and 109th Shinbutai.

As Axtell's division hit the formation, the Japanese aircraft split up and began taking evasive action. In a few minutes of furious action, Axtell shot down five aircraft, which he claimed as 'Vals', sending three down on fire and apparently killing the pilots in the other two aircraft, which spun away into the sea. He damaged three more aircraft during the fighting. Axtell's section leader,

VMF-323's best day came on 22 April when Maj George Axtell (left, squadron CO), Maj Jefferson Dorroh (centre, squadron XO) and 1Lt Jeremiah O'Keefe (right) all became 'aces in a day', collectively shooting down 19 aircraft (*USMCHD*)

1Lt Jeremiah O'Keefe, dropped his flaps to stay with his targets, which he too identified as 'Vals'. O'Keefe shot down four from point-blank range, pulling in directly behind each one before opening fire – all four of his kills burst into flames. O'Keefe's last victory came as he was making a head-on run against an aircraft, pulling up at the last instant as the fatally damaged Japanese aircraft dived into the sea.

Maj Jefferson Dorroh, VMF-323's executive officer, brought his section of three Corsairs into the action shortly after Axtell, and in rapid sequence claimed six aeroplanes shot down and two probably destroyed. Dorrah made most of his kills with high beam attacks, getting hits in the engine and cockpit areas. When the fighting was over VMF-323 had claimed 24.5 Japanese aircraft destroyed, and three pilots – Axtell, Dorrah and O'Keefe – had become 'aces in a day'.

KIKUSUI NO 4 – 27-28 APRIL 1945

For Kikusui Operation No 4, the IJN could marshal only 65 kamikaze aircraft and the JAAF around 50. All the attacks on this day (28 April) were aimed at shipping in and around Okinawa, as the American carriers had drawn out of range to the south. The JAAF's contribution was mostly 26 'Nates' from the 67th, 76th, 77th, 106th, 108th and 109th Shinbutai and six 'Franks' from the 61st Shinbutai, while the IJN sent out 'Kate' and 'Val' Carrier Bombers from the Hachimanshin Chutai, Shirotakaseki Chutai, Dai-ni Seito-tai, Dai-ichi Seki-tai and the Dai-san Sohtei-tai, among other units, with an escort of some 25 Zero-sens. It appears that both the JAAF and the IJN Special Attack missions went out in the afternoon, the latter hoping to arrive over the ships at dusk.

Four divisions of Corsairs from VF-84, flying off *Bunker Hill*, were on CAP at an altitude of 7000 ft near the island of Kikaiga Shima when they saw an enemy formation, which they estimated to consist of 20 'Nates', two 'Tojos' and six 'Franks', approaching 1000 ft above them. The number and composition of this formation bears a close resemblance to the types the JAAF had despatched that day on Special Attack missions.

Climbing to 10,000 ft, the four divisions attacked the Japanese formation from behind, and apparently came in unseen. In their first pass the Corsair pilots shot down six aircraft. The divisions then broke up and pursued the remaining aircraft separately or in sections, claiming 12 more destroyed. In total VF-84 downed 13 'Nates', four 'Franks' and a single 'Tojo', which was probably a misidentified 'Frank'. Lt(jg) John Smith, who had three previous kills with VF-17 and one with VF-84 during the February 1945 strikes on Tokyo, claimed three of the 'Nates' to become an ace. Another ex-VF-17 pilot, Lt Dean 'Chico' Freeman, claimed two of the 'Nates' for his sixth and seventh victories. Lt(jg) Lewis Mayberry, who would become an ace six days later, also claimed a pair of 'Nates'.

Two divisions from VMF-221, VF-84's sister-squadron on *Bunker Hill*, appear to have run into the Zero-sen escort to the IJN's Special Attack mission during a CAP near Izena Shima (Ie Shima) on 28 April. 2Lt Dean Caswell was flying with 1Lt Joseph Brocia Jr and 1Lt John McManus as 'Viceroy 15' at 12,000 ft above a radar picket destroyer when the fighter director called out 'many bogies' coming in from the

Flying with VMF-221 off *Bunker Hill*, 2Lt Dean Caswell was credited with three 'Zekes' destroyed and a fourth as a probable during an intense combat on 28 April. All of Caswell's seven kills during the Okinawa campaign were Zero-sen fighters (*USMCHD*)

Conditions at Kadena and Yontan airfields on Okinawa were rough in the early weeks of the campaign. Alternating dust and mud vied with Japanese artillery to make operations challenging for the Marine Corps Corsair squadrons (*NARA 208-AA-PAC-Box 87-Folder K*)

north at high altitude. Brocia led his division in a maximum power climb up to 20,000 ft.

In the haze that day it was hard for the three pilots to see the enemy aircraft until they were nearly on top of them. Brocia latched onto a 'Zeke' and chased it down, while Caswell found himself in a head-on attack against another 'Zeke'. As Caswell was firing for all he was worth, McManus called out, 'Break right! There's a Zero on your tail!' Caswell could see tracers coming at him from the 'Zeke' ahead of him and going past him from the 'Zeke' on his tail. The fighter in front of him exploded, while the one behind him fell to McManus. Both men then joined up and went after another formation of 'Zekes'. Years later Caswell described this hectic fight in a memoir;

'There seemed to be a hundred enemy fighters in the sky wheeling, climbing and diving in a frantic effort to latch onto three Corsairs. Everywhere I turned I had a shot at one or another. Brocia flashed by smoking a Zero. McManus and I were doing a "Thach Weave" protecting each other and getting some good snap shots into targets. I flamed two more in a row and smoked another, all Zeros. I was feeling so scared I could have thrown up, and had already wet my pants thoroughly.

'An overhead snap shot at the belly of a Zero produced flame and smoke, with several others taking what ammo I had left. My early days of duck shooting would have come in handy if I hadn't been so scared and disoriented. John McManus stayed with me throughout the action, flaming and smoking several that I could see. Thankfully he was protecting my tail. I lost track of Joe Brocia, who was going down hill fast behind a Zero when I saw him last.

'What a melee and, amazingly, the remainder of the Jap fighters reversed course and were gone. My tally was four kills and three probably, and maybe more. McManus thought he had at least three "Zekes" flamed and three probably. Joe Brocia reported two or three. We were very lucky to be alive, and were able to get home safely. My gun camera ran out of film about halfway through the fight, showing only three flamers, so I was

officially credited with three kills and one probably. Who cares? I was alive and my pants could go in the wash.'

Caswell received credit for three 'Zekes', making him an ace, while McManus got four, making him an ace too. The formation VMF-221 attacked may have been from the Sento 312th Hikotai, which sent out 29 Zero-sens and claimed three Corsairs over Ie Shima.

Land-based Marine Corps Corsairs were also in action that day, including a divison of 20 mm cannon-armed F4U-1Cs from VMF-311. 2Lt William Brown was leading these aircraft, which had been scrambled from Yontan airfield and sent to the northeast of Okinawa. Flying at 18,000 ft, Brown saw a formation of eight 'Vals' some 4000 ft below him. Leading his division down into the attack, Brown and his wingman, 2Lt Roland Hamner, pulled in behind a section of 'Vals' and from the 'six o'clock' position opened fire. Brown knocked the wing off his target and Hamner set his on fire.

Climbing back to altitude, Brown saw another 'Val' below him. Diving at his target once again, he made another high-side run from the 'six o'clock' position and shot the 'Val' down in flames for his second victory. VMF-311's Aircraft Action Report noted that 'all pilots were enthusiastic, as usual, about their 20 mm guns'. VMF-323 again did well, Maj Axtell claiming a 'Nate' for his sixth, and final, victory of the war, and 1Lts William Hood and Francis Terrill and 2Lt Dewey Dunford each claiming two aircraft destroyed.

In a month of combat against the kamikaze and conventional aircraft US Navy carrier pilots had claimed 937 Japanese aircraft shot down – 590 of these claims came during the four Kikusui attacks. Carrier- and land-based Marine pilots claimed an additional 279 aircraft. While losses in the air had been low, the kamikaze had hit 108 warships, transports and auxiliary ships, damaging many of the smaller vessels severely. Thirteen ships were sunk or had to be scrapped. It would be another month before the kamikaze attacks began to diminish in intensity.

VMF-311 was the only Marine Corps Corsair squadron on Okinawa to be fully equipped with cannon-armed F4U-1Cs. Despite some operating problems, the unit's pilots were enthusiastic about the destructive power of the 20 mm cannon when used against Japanese fighters (*NARA 127GW-117901*)

2Lt William Brown was VMF-311's sole ace of the Okinawa campaign, claiming two 'Vals' on 28 April, two 'Tonys' and two 'Dinahs' on 4 May and a 'Sonia' on 11 June (*USMCHD*)

THE FINAL BATTLES

The fifth Kokusui attack was scheduled to coincide with a major counterattack by the 32nd Army on Okinawa on 4 May. The JAAF marshalled all the Special Attack aircraft it could muster – around 50 'Nates', 'Oscars', 'Tonys', 'Franks' and 'Nick' fighters – at Chiran airfield. Most of the 11 depleted Special Attack units (19th, 20th, 24th, 42nd, 60th, 66th, 77th, 78th, 105th, 106th and 109th Shinbutai) involved could only contribute a few aircraft to the attack.

The IJN committed 75 mostly obsolete Special Attack aircraft to Kikusui No 5. For the first time it also employed reconnaissance seaplanes as kamikaze aircraft. Three Aichi E13A1 Reconnaissance Seaplanes ('Jakes') and 15 elderly Kawanishi E7K2 Reconnaissance Seaplanes ('Alfs') from the Dai-ichi Kashira-Ku (a maintenance training unit) and the Kotohira Suishin-tai were among the 28 seaplanes that joined a group of Zero-sen and 'Kate' Special Attack aircraft. As before, a force of 35 Shiden-Kai from the 343ed Kokutai sortied on an air superiority mission to clear the area around Kikaiga Shima and Amami Oshima. They shared this mission with 15 JAAF fighters.

The main Special Attack force had an escort of 48 Zero-sen fighters, mostly from the 203rd Kokutai, with an additional 35 JAAF fighters – probably 'Franks' drawn from the 101st, 102nd or 103rd Sentai. For maximum effect all the attacks were concentrated on warships and transports supporting American ground forces fighting on Okinawa. Both the JAAF and IJN attacks began shortly after dawn. For the next several hours an air battle raged north of Okinawa along the route of the kamikaze and over the radar picket ships. Eight US Navy fast carrier squadrons and five land-based Marine Corps Corsair squadrons claimed 167 Japanese aircraft destroyed.

Flying south toward Kikaiga Shima, the Shiden-Kai squadrons of the 343rd Kokutai bounced a division of Hellcats from VBF-12 that had just completed a bombing and strafing run on the island. The Shiden-Kai pilots managed to shoot up the fighter flown by the division leader, Lt W R Jemison. The division immediately began a defensive weave. During this fight Jemison's wingman, Ens Delmar Johannsen, claimed two aircraft shot down. Once again the American pilots misidentified the Shiden-Kai, claiming them as 'Franks', 'Zekes' and 'Tojos'.

Lt Alfred Bolduc brought his division in to support Jemison, seeing 15 Japanese fighters circling below him and peeling off to attack Jemison's Hellcats. Maintaining an altitude advantage and using the sun effectively, Bolduc and his pilots made repeated diving attacks on the Japanese fighters, climbing back up to altitude after each pass. Bolduc claimed four aircraft shot down, which he identified as two 'Franks' and two 'Zekes', to become an ace. The other pilots in his division claimed one each – in total VBF-12 was credited with 12 Japanese fighters shot down. In the battle with VBF-12, the 343rd Kokutai had lost six pilots.

As the formation of kamikaze aircraft headed south, they ran into US Navy and Marine Corps squadrons on CAP. Two divisions from

VF-83 were on CAP over a radar picket near Izena Shima (a small island off Okinawa's northwest coast) when one of them was vectored onto a bogey coming in from the north. Flying in Ens Lyttleton Ward's section, Ens Myron Truax watched as Ward shot down an 'Oscar', then picked off a second Ki-43 attempting to dive on one of the radar picket destroyers.

Separated from his section leader, Truax joined up with three Corsairs that he thought were from a Marine Corps squadron, but which from the action that followed were more likely to have been three F4U-1Cs from VF-85. This flight of four ran into two flights of Type 94 Reconnaissance Seaplanes, which they identified as Type 93 Trainers. Truax attacked one aeroplane in the first flight, hitting it in the cockpit area. The 'Alf' exploded. He continued on and destroyed another in the second flight – the VF-85 pilots shot down five 'Alfs' from this formation. Heading north to re-join his section leader, Truax came across a single 'Val', which he shot down in a head-on attack.

By the time Truax had joined up with Ward, two of the radar pickets had been sunk and the remaining destroyer was pointing out attacking Japanese aircraft to the American CAP by shooting five-inch shells at them. Following these bursts, Ward and Truax found another 'Alf' preparing for an attack. Truax overran it, but Ward managed to shoot the seaplane down after he dropped his wheels and flaps to slow his Hellcat up. Ward's second section managed to join up with him just as another flight of six 'Alfs' appeared to the southeast. The section attacked the seaplanes, who split up and started jinking wildly. Ward also ordered his division to split up and attack the 'Alfs' individually so as to shoot down as many as possible as quickly as possible.

The seaplanes were now flying just above the water, making them a difficult target for the faster Hellcats. Ens Don McPherson, flying as wingman to Lt Carlos Soffe, shot down two, Ward got one for his fourth kill of the day and his fifth kill of the war, while Truax claimed two for his fifth and sixth kills to become an 'ace in a day'. Chasing another group of 'Alfs', McPherson got a third for his fifth kill of the war. Flying to the north, Lt Robert Kincaid of VBF-83 found a 'Sonia', which he shot down with a burst into the fuel tanks, the aeroplane exploding. Thirty minutes later he and his wingman came across three aircraft they identified as 'Vals'. Kincaid shot down three, also becoming an ace.

Lt Eugene Valencia was leading three divisions from VF-9 on a CAP over two radar picket destroyers when they were drawn into the fight against the same large formation of kamikaze aircraft. Vectored out to a contact at 15,000 ft, Valencia climbed up, with Lt Mitchell as his wingman, leaving Lt French and Lt(jg) Smith on station. Finding nothing, Valencia and Mitchell were descending to join up with French and Smith when they saw a 'Frank' and a 'Dinah' (which may

'Valencia's Flying Circus' was the name VF-9 gave to Lt Eugene Valencia's division on board *Yorktown*. Valencia had trained the members of his division in his own mutual supportive tactics, which proved highly effective. Pilots within the division claimed a combined tally of 36.5 victories during the Okinawa campaign – 20 of these during two missions on 4 and 11 May – and they finished the war with 50 kills in total. The members of 'Valencia's Flying Circus' were, from left to right, Lt(jg)s Harris Mitchell, Clifton Smith, James French and Lt Eugene Valencia (*NARA 80G-700016*)

have actually been one of the 'Nicks' the 24th Shinbutai had sent out that morning). Valencia downed the 'Frank' and Mitchell claimed the 'Dinah'/'Nick'.

After the division reformed they saw a larger formation of Japanese aircraft coming down from the north at altitudes from 3000 ft down to the sea, many carrying one or two bombs. Some kamikaze aeroplanes were already making their dives onto the picket ships, while other friendly fighters were heavily engaged in attempting to fend them off. In a rapid sequence of combats, sometimes on their own and sometimes together, Valencia and his division claimed 11.5 aeroplanes shot down. Valencia claimed 1.5 'Franks' and two 'Vals' shot down, while Lt Harris Mitchell downed two 'Franks' in addition to his 'Dinah'/'Nick', these kills making him an ace. Lt James French claimed an 'Oscar', a 'Frank' and a 'Nate' for his fifth, sixth and seventh kills, while Lt(jg) Clinton Smith added a 'Frank' and a 'Judy' to his total.

VMF-323 had sent up four divisions from Kadena airfield at 0730 hrs on a CAP north of Okinawa. Around 30 minutes later the fighter directors began picking up bogies as the large kamikaze formation approached. It sent each of the divisions to a different position to intercept them. Leading one division, 1Lt Joseph Dillard and his wingman came across several aircraft that they identified as 'Dinahs' and 'Vals'. Dillard downed two 'Dinahs' and a 'Val', and shared another 'Dinah' and a 'Val' with his wingman, giving him five victories in total to make ace. Lt Francis Terrill, Dillard's section leader, came in on the same formation, claiming 1.25 'Dinahs' and a 'Val' shot down, with two more 'Dinahs' and two 'Vals' damaged.

2Lts John Ruhsam and Robert Wade had remained on station when their division leader had to escort his wingman back to base. In the combat that followed the two young 2Lts narrowly missed becoming 'aces in a day'. Spotting a single 'Val', Ruhsam and Wade gave chase, running into a formation of 25 aircraft they identified as 'Nates' and 'Vals', but which may well have been an all-JAAF formation of 'Nates' and 'Sonias'. The Japanese aeroplanes were milling around at 4000 ft when Ruhsam and Wade attacked. Making beam runs, Ruhsam shot down four 'Vals' and damaged three more. Wade put in claims for two 'Vals' and two 'Nates' destroyed and three 'Nates' damaged. These victories made both pilots aces.

VMF-323 pilots claimed 24.75 aircraft shot down during the day. Several pilots noted in VMF-323's Aircraft Action Report that the 'Dinahs' appeared to be making torpedo runs on the ships, which means that the twin-engined aeroplanes VMF-323 downed may have been JAAF 'Peggy' bombers from the 7th or 98th Sentai, which were trained for torpedo attacks.

Then 2Lts John Ruhsam and Robert Wade and 1Lt Joseph Dillard stand next to a blackboard recording MAG-33 and MAG-31 victories for 22 April 1945. The arrow points to VMF-323's score of 24.5 kills. On 4 May these three pilots contributed 11 victories to VMF-323's total, narrowly missing becoming 'aces in a day'. VMF-323 was the highest-scoring Marine Corps squadron of the Okinawa campaign with 124.5 victories (*NARA 80G-373359*)

By late morning the main attack was over. It had been a costly few hours for the US Navy as the kamikaze had managed to hit 16 ships, sinking two destroyers and two LCM(R)s on picket duty. Late in the afternoon 2Lt William Brown of VMF-311 led a division on a CAP north of Okinawa. After 90 minutes on patrol, Brown received a call to intercept incoming bogies to the southwest. Reaching the intercept point, the division saw a formation of 11 aircraft they identified as eight 'Tonys' and three twin-engined 'Dinahs' heading for the invasion fleet anchorage at Kerema Retto. This may actually have been a mixed formation of four 'Tonys' from the 19th and 105th Sentai, based on Formosa, with a number of 'Franks' from the 34th and 120th Shinbutai, which sent off nine fighters on this day, and some 'Nicks' from the 123rd Shinbutai, also from Formosa.

Diving through scattered clouds in the dusk, Brown led his division in a turn to come in on the Japanese formation from the rear, arriving in a firing position undetected. All four pilots managed to shoot down an aircraft, which they each claimed as a 'Tony', on this first pass. The division then broke up into individual combats. Brown shot down a second 'Tony', with hits to the left wing and fuselage, using only two of his 20 mm cannon. He then took on two of the twin-engined aircraft and shot down both with rear attacks, again using only two of his cannon. These four kills made Brown an ace. Together, his division shot down the entire Japanese formation using 1500 rounds of 20 mm ammunition out of 3520 rounds available – an average of just 136 rounds per kill.

As the Aircraft Action Report noted once again, 'enthusiasm on the part of the pilots for their 20 mm guns, which functioned perfectly throughout, was boundless. Each one reported that the Jap aeroplanes, when hit, seemed to partially or totally disintegrate, with large pieces of fuselage, wing or engine flying off in all directions'.

KIKUSUI NO 6 – 10-11 MAY 1945

Despite the claims for a significant number of naval vessels sunk or damaged through the kamikaze attacks, the Japanese high command could find no evidence that the American hold on Okinawa was weakening. To the contrary, US forces appeared to be rapidly expanding the number of airfields on the island and bringing in more land-based air support. While still sending out Special Attack units against the American carriers, the Combined Fleet headquarters ordered a renewed effort against shipping off Okinawa that was supporting the invasion.

A significant problem was the declining number of fighters available to escort the kamikaze to Okinawa. For Kikusui Operation No 6, the IJN prepared a mixed force of 18 'Judys' and 26 Zero-sen fighters from the 721st Kokutai for an attack on the carrier groups (in the event only the Zero-sens undertook the mission), while another combined force of ten 'Jills', eight P1Y2-S 'Frances' nightfighters, five Zero-sens and two reconnaissance seaplanes (an 'Alf' and a 'Jake'), with four Ohka-carrying 'Bettys', headed for shipping around Okinawa, with an escort of 65 Zero-sen fighters from the 203rd and 252nd Kokutai and other fighter units as escort. The 6th Army Air Force committed seven 'Peggy' bombers, 15 'Franks' as escort and 36 Special Attack aeroplanes ('Oscars', 'Nates', 'Tonys' and 'Franks') drawn from 12 Special Attack units.

On the morning of 11 May Lt Eugene Valencia was once again leading three divisions of VF-9 Hellcats on a CAP. Reporting in to the fighter director, Valencia was ordered to take his division to orbit near the island of Yoron Shima, north of Okinawa. The second division, under Lt Marvin Franger, was sent 20 miles beyond Valencia, and Lt Bert Eckard's division headed 30 miles west of Izema Shima. Valencia's division spotted a formation of JAAF fighters consisting of what they identified as 'Tonys', 'Oscars', 'Franks' and 'Tojos' already fighting with US Navy Hellcats and Corsairs.

In the fight that followed the division became separated. Fighting on his own or linking up with Hellcats from another squadron, Valencia claimed a 'Tojo', an 'Oscar' and an unidentified JAAF fighter (probably a 'Frank'), and a 'Zeke' as a probable, for his last kills of the war, taking his score to 23. Lt(jg) Mitchell had three 'Tonys' jump him, and he had to split-S to get away. Seeing several 'Tonys' with Corsairs chasing them, Mitchell dove down and shot one into the sea, getting a second after a long chase. Lt James French and Lt(jg) Clinton Smith managed to stay together, French claiming an 'Oscar' and two 'Franks' in the general melee. After rejoining with Valencia when the fight was over, Smith sighted a 'Frances' and gave chase as it headed for a radar picket ship. He got hits in the port engine, which began to burn. The 'Frances' crashed into the sea and blew up just 1000 yards from the destroyer.

Out to the west, Lt Eckard's division sighted a group of seven 'Zekes' at 20,000 ft. His section leader dived down to attack another gaggle below, leaving Eckard and his wingman, Ens Joseph Kaelin, going after the seven. This formation turned out to be part of a larger group of 30 to 35 'Zekes' without bombs – most likely part of the escort force for the IJN's Special Attack aircraft.

Beginning with an attack on stragglers at the rear of the formation, Eckard and Kaelin kept an altitude advantage as the Japanese formation

The pilots of Sento 303rd Hikotai had the difficult task of escorting the IJN Special Attack units on their sorties against the American fleet. On most missions the escorts were hard put to save themselves from destruction, much less shepherd their charges to the target (*Jack Lambert Collection, Museum of Flight*)

Lt Bert Eckard of VF-9 ran into a group of Zero-sen escorts on 11 May, claiming five of them shot down during the mission to add to his two previous victories, earning him the Navy Cross for his efforts (*NARA 80G-329442*)

broke up into defensive turns and dives, apparently unable to locate their attackers among so many aircraft. After each run the two Hellcat pilots climbed back up to altitude to begin again. They kept up the attacks for around 20 minutes, Eckard claiming five 'Zekes' shot down and another damaged to become an 'ace in a day', while Kaelin narrowly missed this accolade with three 'Zekes' destroyed, a probable and two damaged. Collectively, the three VF-9 divisions claimed 20 aircraft shot down.

Flying an early morning CAP near Kikai Shima, two divisions from VF-84 also ran into the JAAF Special Attack force. The Corsairs were at 8000 ft when they saw two formations of Japanese aircraft flying some 3000 ft below them. Lts Doris 'Chico' Freeman and John M Smith, both veterans of VF-17 in the Solomons, led their divisions down on a group of 'Nate' fighters in one of the formations. In a one-sided contest the VF-84 pilots shot down seven 'Nates' in a matter of minutes, Freeman getting one and Smith two on their first pass. Smith then found a fighter he identified as a 'Zeke' and shot it down too.

Returning to *Bunker Hill*, 'Chico' Freeman and 21 other VF-84 pilots were sitting in their ready room when, shortly after 1000 hrs, two Zero-sen kamikaze hit the carrier one after the other. A bomb from one of the aircraft penetrated the ready room area, killing Freeman and the other pilots around him – Smith survived. The damage was severe, killing 393 men and knocking *Bunker Hill* out of the war.

——— KIKUSUI NO 7 – 24-25 MAY 1945 ———

Kikusui Operation No 7 was the last mass kamikaze attack in significant numbers, the IJN marshalling 65 kamikaze aircraft and the JAAF 100. Subsequent attacks would see a steadily diminishing number of kamikaze aircraft employed. A lack of aircraft, attacks on airfields (between 17 April and 11 May B-29s of the Twentieth Air Force bombed 17 airfields on Kyushu and Shikoku) and poor weather caused the two-week gap between Kikusui No 6 and Kikusui No 7. Both the JAAF and the IJN were running short of aeroplanes and pilots for Special Attack and conventional missions. The IJN in particular was facing a shortage of fighters for both air defence and escort missions. Having suffered heavy losses in the aerial battles of 11 May, it took more time to prepare aeroplanes and pilots for the next mass attack.

On 13 May TF 58 began two days of strikes against the airfields on Kyushu, sending in three waves of fighters and bombers. On the first day of strikes the Japanese put up a minimal defence, the carrier pilots claiming only nine aircraft shot down.

The following day there were more combats over Kyushu, and while defending the task force several pilots became aces during the course of the day. In a mid-afternoon strike on Kushira airfield on Kyushu, Lt Jim Pearce was leading a division from VF-17 and one from VBF-17 when, just after finishing their attack on the base, they heard a 'tally ho' call from VF-82 pilots flying over Kagoshima Bay. Lt(jg) Carl Van Stone, flying in Lt Moore's VBF-17 division, spotted a lone 'Frank' heading north up the bay. The division gave chase and then found itself under attack from several formations of 'Franks' that bounced them out of the overcast. Stone went after a 'Frank' that had overshot him, sending it down smoking. He and his wingman then attacked two 'Franks' that had made an attack on the division and again overshot, sending them down on fire. These two kills made Stone an ace, and he and his wingman damaged two more during the fight. Lt Jim Pearce also claimed a 'Frank' for his fifth, and final, kill. Finally, VF-82's Lt Robert Jennings despatched a 'Tony' over the bay for his sixth, and last, victory.

Late in the afternoon 13 Corsairs from VBF-83 were on a sweep over airfields in northeastern Kyushu when they saw two 'Jake' floatplanes and two 'Zekes' across the inland sea near Honshu. Lt Thomas Reidy and his wingman went after them, the former shooting one down for his last claim of the Okinawa campaign. Lt Lindley Godson targeted one of the 'Jakes', getting hits in the engine and sending it down to crash for his fifth, and last, kill of the war. VF-30 also participated in the airfield strikes, sending out 14 Hellcats armed with 500-lb bombs to hit Kokubu and Ronchi airfields at the northern end of Kagoshima Bay.

Ens Austen Olsen's bombs failed to release during his dive on Kokubu, but when he pulled out of his dive he saw an aircraft ahead of him, which he identified as a 'Jack'. With his bombs still attached, Olsen and his wingman went after the Japanese fighter at full throttle. Olsen fired off a short burst from 3000 ft in the hope that the Japanese pilot would start an evasive manoeuvrer which he did, turning sharply to the left. This gave the Hellcat pilot the chance to rapidly catch the 'Jack', hitting the aeroplane in both wings with several bursts. The IJN fighter did a wingover and crashed into a hill for Olsen's fifth victory.

Japanese reconnaissance aeroplanes had located TF 58 southeast of Kyushu. Early in the morning the IJN sent out a force of 28 Special

F6F-5 Hellcats taking off from the USS *Randolph* (CV-15) during May 1945. VF-12 and its sister-squadron VBF-12 used the Hellcats on board interchangeably (*Jack Lambert Collection, Museum of Flight*)

VBF-12 produced two aces during the Okinawa campaign. Ens Delmar Johannsen became an ace in only two missions, claiming two 'Zekes' on 4 May and three more ten days later (*American Fighter Aces Association, Museum of Flight*)

Attack aircraft, including 22 Zero-sens from the 721st Kokutai, with a Zero-sen fighter escort. Ens Delmar Johannsen was flying as part of a three-Hellcat division from VBF-12 on a CAP north of the Task Force when his division saw eight bomb-carrying 'Zekes', most likely from the 721st Kokutai, orbiting the task force's destroyer screen at 20,000 ft. Johannsen and his division leader, Lt William Jemison, dove after two of the Zekes that had peeled off from the formation, shooting both of them down in flames. Johannsen then saw a formation of three 'Zekes', which he attacked on his own, shooting down two more in flames for his fourth and fifth kills.

During the morning, however, a kamikaze managed to break through the CAP and hit *Enterprise*, blowing up the forward elevator and sending the veteran carrier home for repairs.

Scheduled for 23 May, Kikusui Operation No 7 had to be postponed for two days due to poor weather over the home islands and then over Okinawa. The IJN managed to pull together 65 Special Attack aircraft consisting principally of 'Frances' and 'Vals', with an escort of Zero-sens. The 6th Air Army brought together 100 Special Attack aircraft – the second-highest number sent out during the ten Kikusui attacks.

For this attack the 6th Air Army committed some 33 'Franks' from the 26th, 57th, 58th, 60th, 61st Shinbutai and the 62nd Sentai, ten 'Tonys' from the 54th, 55th and 56th Shinbutai, some 15 'Oscars', at least seven 'Nicks' and a number of elderly 'Nates'. No fewer than 20 of these aircraft had to return to their base at Chiran for various reasons, however.

The objective of the mass attack, which left Kyushu early in the morning, was shipping around Okinawa rather than the American carrier force, then withdrawing south after strikes on Kyushu airfields the day before. Marine Corps Corsair squadrons based on Okinawa, recently reinforced with a new MAG and the first USAAF fighter group to join the Tactical Air Force, took on the kamikaze attack. Marine Corps pilots claimed 42 Japanese aircraft shot down and their USAAF counterparts 34. The cost was 12 ships attacked, of which two were sunk.

Early that morning Capt Herbert Valentine had led a division from VMF-312 some 60 miles north of Okinawa as part of a 60-aeroplane CAP. When his division was relieved, he asked permission to stay on patrol and head farther north, which was granted. Flying at 3000 ft, Valentine soon spotted a 'Zeke' at 1500 ft. At the same time his section leader, 1Lt William Farrell, saw a formation of 15 bomb-carrying 'Zekes' coming in from the north. Valentine attacked the 'Zeke' below him while Farrell and his wingman, 2Lt John Read, took on the larger formation. Valentine shot the 'Zeke' down on his first pass, then climbed back up to join Farrell. He and Read each downed a 'Zeke' on their first pass too, but Valentine's wingman, 2Lt Malcom Birney, who had shot down a 'Zeke' on his first pass at the formation, became involved in a dogfight

VMF-312's Corsairs carried a distinctive chequerboard marking on the cowl and rudder. The Marine Corps Corsair squadrons flew close air support missions when not on CAPs. This Corsair is being armed with eight HVARs and two 500-lb bombs (*USMCHD*)

with a second 'Zeke' which shot him down. The fight with the 'Zekes' continued for around ten minutes, Valentine claiming two more shot down and a probable, while Farrell destroyed one and shared a second with Read. As the fight was ending a formation of P-47Ns from the newly arrived 318th FG joined in.

Pulling away, Valentine saw six aircraft he identified as three 'Tojos' and three 'Vals' (these may in fact have been JAAF 'Franks' and 'Nates' from the 6th Air Army's formation). Valentine quickly shot down two of the aircraft he thought were 'Tojos' and one of the 'Vals', sharing a second with 2Lt Read, while Farrell destroyed the third 'Tojo' and the third 'Val'. With his 5.5 victories, Capt Valentine became the last Marine Corps 'ace in a day' of World War 2. Having begun the day with credit for a shared kill on 16 April 1945, 1Lt Farrell's 4.5 victories made him an ace as well.

One other Marine achieved acedom on this day too. Capt Floyd Kirkpatrick of VMF-441 was leading a division of four Corsairs on one of the early morning CAPs when he noticed AAA from friendly ships below bursting over Yagaji Island, just off the west central coast of Okinawa. Flying towards the scene, Kirkpatrick saw a Japanese aircraft with a bomb under its left wing heading southeast toward American ships. Kirkpatrick identified the aeroplane as a 'Zeke', but since the then-current model (A6M5) of the Zero-sen fighter had no underwing attachment points, this fighter may have been a JAAF 'Oscar' or 'Frank'.

The four Corsairs initiated an attack on the 'Zeke', which for once began to take violent evasive action, suggesting a more experienced pilot was at the controls. Kirkpatrick pushed his Corsair down through the intense AAA and caught the 'Zeke' as it was entering a dive, getting hits in the cockpit area and the engine. The aircraft caught fire and crashed into the sea for Kirkpatrick's fifth victory.

The 318th FG began arriving on the island of Ie Shima, off the west coast of Okinawa, on 13 May. Within a week the group's three

The P-47Ns of the 318th FG's three squadrons arrived on the island of Ie Shima, off the coast of Okinawa, on 14-15 May and began operations shortly thereafter (*NARA 342FH 3A-4021*)

A formation of P-47Ns heads out on a mission while an aircraft from the 19th FS gets its engine worked on (*NARA 342FH 3A-4447*)

squadrons – 19th, 73rd and 333rd FSs – had 100+ new P-47Ns on the ground and had begun flying CAPs around Okinawa and strike and heckler missions to Kyushu.

On 25 May the 19th and 73rd FSs sent out 28 P-47Ns at 0630 hrs to bomb and strafe several airfields on Kyushu. En route the formation ran into extremely bad weather and had to abort the mission, jettisoning their bombs and turning back to base. 1Lt Richard Anderson of the 19th FS was leading an element in 'Cossack 101' flight, with 2Lt Donald Kennedy as his wingman, when they became separated from their flight leader. Letting down from 14,000 ft to the deck, they came out at the

75

southern tip of Amami Shima to find approximately 30 Japanese aircraft flying in loose V formations at 2000 ft. They identified these as 'Zekes', although as the combat report states that the aeroplanes were equipped with wing tanks, these may actually have been the 6th Air Army's formation of 'Franks' that were similar in number.

Anderson attacked immediately, shooting down one 'Zeke' in a head-on pass. Coming around, he closed with a second 'Zeke' and shot it down from behind, quickly moving on to a third and firing a five-second burst that sent the fighter crashing into the sea. Anderson then attacked a fourth 'Zeke' in another stern attack, the fighter starting to smoke and eventually rolling over and hitting the water. He despatched his fifth 'Zeke' with a 30-degree deflection shot, and was lining up his sixth when his ammunition ran out. Anderson noted in the combat report that none of the 'Zekes' he attacked took evasive action apart from gentle turns. As well as becoming an 'ace in a day', Anderson became the first ace in the 318th FG.

On a CAP that same morning Anderson's squadronmate 1Lt Stanley Lustic and his flight came across six 'Oscars' flying north of Okinawa. Lustic quickly shot down three of them, none taking evasive action, for his first kills of the war.

KIKUSUI No 8 – 27-28 MAY 1945

Kikusui Operation No 8 involved 60 IJN and 50 JAAF Special Attack aircraft, including, for the first time, Army Type 2 Advanced Trainers, which had little chance of survival against American fighters. The attacks on 27-28 May managed to hit 14 American ships, sinking one destroyer. Over the two days Marine Corps fighter pilots claimed 31 Japanese

1Lt. Richard Anderson (left) was the 318th FG's first 'ace in a day'. He flew with the 19th FS and shot down five 'Zekes' on 25 May – the only time Anderson encountered Japanese aircraft in combat (*Jack Lambert Collection, Museum of Flight*)

1Lt Stanley Lustic also became an ace on 28 May. Having scored three victories on 25 May, Lustic added two more on the 28th flying his P-47N *STANLEY'S STEAMER* (*Photograph courtesy of Jack Lambert*)

aircraft shot down, although none of the pilots involved were, or became, aces. On the 28th Lt Edgar McClure of VBF-9 destroyed a 'Frances' to become the squadron's sole ace.

That same day two USAAF pilots from the 19th FS managed to achieve this title in two separate missions over Kyushu. During the morning the unit sent off 12 P-47Ns on a heckling mission over the Kanyoa airfields on Kyushu – two had to abort, but the others continued on the mission. Flying over Kanoya airfield at 13,000 ft, the Thunderbolts observed nine 'Zekes' taking off from Kanoya East airfield. Maj De Jack Williams, leading the mission that day, shot at a 'Zeke' after diving on the formation, then climbed back up to rejoin the others, ordering another pass over the airfield. At this point 1Lt William Mathis called out bogies approaching from the northeast, which he identified as 'Zekes'. These aircraft were actually part of a formation of 20 'Georges' from the 343rd Kokutai climbing to intercept the American fighters.

In the dogfight that followed the Japanese pilots proved to be very aggressive, and resorted to vigorous evasive action to avoid their attackers. Nevertheless, the P-47N's superior performance at altitude enabled the American pilots to prevail. When four of the 'Georges' attacked Lt Stanley Lustic's flight leader, Lustic went after them immediately. Two of the 'Georges' dove away, but Lustic opened fire on

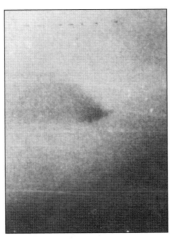

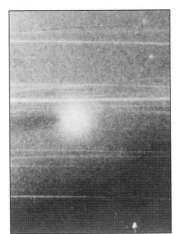

This sequence from the gun camera of a pilot off *Bennington* illustrates what could happen when a Japanese fighter received a full burst of 0.50-cal shells from a Hellcat or Corsair. Pilots often noted in the Aircraft Action Report that their targets exploded in a ball of flame (*NARA USS Bennington After Action Report*)

one of the two that remained, getting hits and knocking pieces off the fuselage. The 'George' burst into flame and crashed. The second fighter fell away in a split-S, with Lustic following, setting it on fire. These two claims brought Lustic's total to five aircraft in two missions.

1Lt Mathis then engaged another formation of 'Georges' that was also coming in from the northeast. Swinging wide to come in behind them, Mathis open fired once he was in range and watched a Japanese fighter explode. He then pulled in behind another 'George' and caused this aircraft to explode as well. Finally, and despite all but one of his guns having stopped firing, he targeted yet another fighter. Another pilot saw this 'George' explode, giving Mathis three claims for the day.

That afternoon the 19th FS sent another 12 P-47Ns to Kyushu, although on this mission five aircraft aborted. Capt John Vogt led the rest to the airfields around Kanoya where he saw a formation of 28 'Zekes' approaching from the northwest. They started to form a large circle above the P-47s, but before they could complete the move Vogt led his flight into a climb, the 'Zekes' following. Using war emergency power, the Thunderbolt pilots reached 28,000 ft – about 1000 ft above the 'Zeke' formation, which proceeded to break up. Some dived away and some remained at altitude in sections of two.

Vogt dived after one of the 'Zekes', which exploded under his fire. Continuing a shallow dive, Vogt came in behind another 'Zeke', which also exploded after a short burst of fire. Vogt and his wingman then attacked one of the elements of two 'Zekes', the former shooting down the wingman and then targeting the leader of the element, setting his fighter on fire as well. Minutes later Vogt shot at another 'Zeke' that had tried to pull up into him, getting hits but failing to see the result. Another 'Zeke' began a pass at Vogt, and the two aeroplanes raced at each other head on. The 'Zeke' pilot did not waiver, but fortunately for Vogt the Japanese fighter blew up under the weight of fire from his eight 0.50-cal machine guns.

Capt John Vogt, also with the 19th FS, became an 'ace in a day' three days after 1Lt Richard Anderson. Vogt is shown here with his P-47N *DRINK'N SISTER* (*Photograph courtesy of Jack Lambert*)

The P-47 pilots observed that some of their opponents during this engagement had 'used excellent judgment and displayed good flying ability', but employed poor tactics. The pilots felt that the P-47N completely outperformed the 'Zeke' at high altitude, even allowing them to out-turn and out-climb the more manoeuvrable Japanese fighter.

KIKUSUI NO 9 – 3-7 JUNE 1945

As the Kikusui operations came to an end, the number of kamikaze aircraft involved dropped sharply. Postponed several days because of weather, Kikusui Operation No 9 began on 3 June. The IJN could muster only 20 Special Attack aircraft, mostly 'Vals', while the JAAF sent out 30 aircraft, again consisting mostly of 'Nates'. The IJN sent out a force of 65 Zero-sen fighters as escort. While the Fast Carrier Task Force (now designated TF 38 after Adm William Halsey took over from Adm Raymond Spruance on 27 May) made regular strikes on the Kyushu airfields, the Marine Corps Corsair and JAAF Thunderbolt squadrons took over responsibility for the air defence of Okinawa, combining CAPs north of the island with regular fighter sweeps over Kyushu.

On 3 June Marine Corps pilots claimed 33 Japanese aircraft shot down. VMF-323 pilots accounted for 15 of them during three CAPs. Flying just such a mission 20 miles west of the island of Iheya Shima, northwest of Okinawa, a division of four Corsairs ran into part of the Zero-sen. The Marine Corps pilots quickly discovered that their opponents on this occasion were far from novices. Indeed, the Aircraft Action Report commented that 'all "Zekes" encountered were very aggressive, and they experienced no trouble out-manoeuvring the Corsairs at slow speeds'.

The VMF-323 division was flying at 13,000 ft when the pilots were given a vector and told to climb to 20,000 ft. Breaking through the overcast, 1Lt Cyril Dolezel, leading the division, spotted a formation of 25 'Zekes' at 20,000 ft. Seeing the Corsairs below them, the IJN pilots came down to attack. 1Lt Charles Drake, Dolezel's wingman, lost his leader in the melee that followed. On his own, Drake went after a section of 'Zekes' he saw at 17,000 ft. Closing in from below, Drake fired on one of the 'Zekes' from 'five o'clock', getting hits in the cockpit area.

This combat-weary Corsair flew with VMF-323, but it bears evidence of having previously flown off *Bunker Hill* – note that the vessel's arrow geometric marking has been painted out on the tail and starboard wing (*Jack Lambert Collection, Museum of Flight*)

As the two 'Zekes' made a turn to the right, Drake's target erupted in flames. He then fired on the second 'Zeke', again from a position below and to the right, setting it on fire as well.

Seeing another formation of three 'Zekes', Drake came in behind the tail end aircraft and shot it down in flames, overshooting the other two fighters as he did so. They immediately got on his tail. Diving in order to use the Corsair's superior speed, Drake managed to pull away. Coming around in a right-hand turn, he came back up underneath the two 'Zekes' and fired on the rear aircraft, setting it on fire, and then sent a burst into the leader, who started smoking prior to diving into the overcast. Drake received credit for four 'Zekes' destroyed and one probable, making him an ace. Drake received the Navy Cross for his skilful flying and shooting. In the same battle 1Lt Albert Wells claimed two 'Zekes' for his fourth and fifth kills.

1Lt Stuart Alley and 2Lt Dewey Durnford were flying as part of a three-aeroplane division on a CAP to the east of Okinawa when they ran into a number of 'Vals' and a single 'Nate' fighter. When his division leader overshot on his pass on a single 'Val' flying at 500 ft, Alley came in and opened fire at 300 yards from behind, hitting the dive-bomber in the cockpit area and sending it down into the sea. Seeing a formation of five 'Vals', the division gave chase. Alley came in behind one of the aircraft, and after hitting the 'Val' in the fuselage it exploded. He then attacked a second, which also erupted in flames and crashed into the sea. 2Lt Durnford came in behind one of the remaining 'Vals' that was trying to escape in a diving turn. Durnford followed, opening fire at 250 yards. As with the others, the 'Val' exploded in flames and crashed into the sea.

2Lt Stuart Alley of VMF-323 became an ace on 3 June when he claimed three 'Vals'. Alley made all his claims during three missions between 17 May and 3 June (*Jack Lambert Collection*)

Pulling up, Durnford saw a single 'Nate' flying at 2000 ft above him and opened fire. The JAAF fighter did a split-S, then pulled up in a climbing turn. Durnford came in again and hit the 'Nate' from below, sending the Japanese fighter spinning down into the water. Alley and Durnford both became aces on this mission.

Three days later, on 6 June, Capt Judge Wolfe, a flight leader in the 333rd FS, obtained one of the most remarkable victories of the Okinawa campaign. Wolfe was leading a flight on a fighter sweep over southern Kyushu, the 318th FG having sent out elements from all three units. As the HVAR-equipped P-47Ns headed over Kagoshima Bay, Wolfe saw seven 'Zekes' flying at 25,000 ft some 20 miles to the north. Wolfe turned his flight to the right and climbed up to 25,000 ft so as to bounce the Japanese fighters from behind.

Alley's squadronmate 2Lt Dewey Durnford also became an ace on 3 June. Having scored 4.333 victories during April, Durnford went through a scoring drought in May before getting his fifth, and final, victory (*USMCHD*)

Approaching apparently undetected, Wolfe dived down on the left hand element of two 'Zekes'. From a range of 1000-1200 ft immediately behind one of aircraft, he fired off the four HVARs he was carrying and the 'Zeke' exploded when the rockets hit home. Quickly pulling in behind the element leader, Wolfe opened fire at 900 ft and closed in, getting hits on the wings, cockpit area and fuselage. The 'Zeke' burst into flames and went spinning down. These kills made Wolfe an ace.

Four days later, on 10 June, Wolfe was leading a flight on another combined fighter sweep over Kyushu. Flying at high altitude, three flights of P-47Ns dropped 'window' radar decoy strips off the coast of Kyushu as a diversion for a photographic mission by US Navy PB4Y-2 aircraft. Dropping down to a lower altitude, they spotted a formation of nine 'Zekes' below them. Wolfe led his flight into the formation in a stern attack, closing in on one of the 'Zekes' and opening fire from 800 ft, knocking the Zero-sen's wing off. He then closed in on another 'Zeke', again opening fire from very close range and getting hits in the cockpit

Capt Judge Wolfe's P-47N on 12 June 1945, showing his final wartime tally of nine victories. Wolfe claimed seven Japanese aircraft flying out of Ie Shima during May-June 1945 (*Photograph courtesy of Jack Lambert*)

1Lt William Mathis was the 19th FS's fourth, and last, ace of the Okinawa campaign. Flying P-47N *BOTTOMS' UP*, Mathis shot down three 'Oscars' on 28 May and added two 'Zekes' on 22 June for his final victories (*Photograph courtesy of Jack Lambert*)

area. Moments later he watched the pilot bail out. Reforming after the fight, the P-47 pilots headed north of Kagoshima Bay, climbing to 23,000 ft.

North of the bay Wolfe saw a large formation of around 50 Japanese fighters that he identified as 'Jacks' at an altitude of 30,000 ft. This may have been a mixed formation from the 302nd, 332nd and 352nd Kokutai, all of which were equipped with the J2M Raiden and had units based in Kyushu to intercept the B-29 raids. Climbing to 32,000 ft above the Japanese formation, as Wolfe was setting up his attack the 'Jacks' began diving away from the Thunderbolts. Wolfe gave chase, closing in on a 'Jack' and setting it on fire from close range. He then targeted a second J2M, sending the fighter down with its cockpit and central wing area on fire for his fourth kill of the mission.

KIKUSUI No 10 – 21-22 JUNE 1945

The final Kikusui attack was delayed due to weather (June is the rainy season in Japan). The attack was scheduled for 14 June, but it was initially put back 48 hours and then postponed indefinitely. Finally, on 21 June, the weather cleared sufficiently for Kikusui Operation No 10 to begin. For this last attack against US naval vessels off Okinawa the IJN could send only 30 Special Attack aircraft and the JAAF just 15. The operation itself was pointless, as by this time the battle for Okinawa was effectively over, but it went ahead nonetheless.

The 721st Kokutai flew its last Ohka mission to Okinawa on this date, sending off six 'Betty' bombers with a strong escort of 65 Zero-sens. Three of the bombers had to turn back with mechanical problems, leaving the remaining three to be shot down. Marine Corps Corsair pilots claimed 28 Japanese aircraft destroyed, while their USAAF counterparts in the 318th FG bagged 11.

The next day's combat brought one last pilot the title of ace. Lt William Mathis was on a CAP with other 19th FS pilots off Amami Shima when three 'Zekes' were observed at 0730 hrs flying in a loose formation below the

Thunderbolts at an altitude of 300-400 ft. Flight leader Maj Charles Tennant dived on one of the 'Zekes', setting it on fire with a short burst. Mathis went after the other two 'Zekes', one pilot making very tight turns in a forlorn attempt to evade him – Mathis hit this 'Zeke' with a 90-degree deflection shot. The second fighter took no evasive action, the pilot being either inexperienced or resigned to his fate. Mathis sent the 'Zeke' flaming into the sea with a stern attack for his fifth, and final victory, of the war. None of the Thunderbolt pilots bothered to jettison their drop tanks during their attack. Organised fighting on Okinawa ended on 22 June.

Pilots and groundcrewmen watch as the 19th FS's scoreboard is mounted above a hangar, showing 70 victories, 60 of which were claimed during the Okinawa campaign (*NARA 3A-4478*)

NIGHTFIGHTERS AND NEAR ACES

When the United States entered the war, neither the US Navy nor the Marine Corps had any aerial nightfighting capability. A crash programme led to the development of radar-equipped single-seat nightfighters that could operate from aircraft carriers or land bases. Both the US Navy and the Marine Corps adopted the F6F Hellcat as their standard nightfighter, the F6F-5N version entering service in the autumn of 1944. Over the next 12 months the US Navy activated 25 nightfighter squadrons and the Marine Corps activated eight, although only a small number saw action.

With the formation of the first night air group in August 1944, and the decision not to employ squadron-strength nightfighter units in the frontline, the US Navy now had an excess of nightfighter units and pilots. Most of the squadrons were disbanded and the pilots and aeroplanes used to form small detachments called Night Fighter Units, each with four F6F-5Ns, six to eight pilots and a nightfighter director. The Night Fighter Units were assigned to regular US Navy fighter squadrons on board the larger *Essex*-class carriers. During the Okinawa campaign 11 carriers had attached Night Fighter Units. Once airfields on Okinawa had been prepared, the MAGs brought in three Marine Corps nightfighter squadrons too. Five nightfighter pilots – four US Navy and one Marine Corps – became aces during the campaign.

During the invasion of Okinawa the IJN regularly sent out reconnaissance aircraft at dusk, during the night and at dawn to locate and track the American carrier groups – the primary target for the Special Attack units. Fast Saiun Carrier Reconnaissance Aircraft ('Myrt') usually performed this hazardous mission, although Army Type 100 Reconnaissance Aircraft ('Dinah') were also occasionally used too.

Following the landings in early April, the IJN and the JAAF began sending out both conventional and Special Attack aircraft at night to attack American shipping and the airfields on Okinawa. Kadena and Yontan were subject to almost nightly bombing and heckling attacks from small numbers of Japanese aeroplanes that would circle off the coast before coming in singly to make their bombing runs. In response, carrier- and land-based nightfighters flew patrols during the

Several nightfighter units painted over the geometric fleet carrier identification markings to reduce the visibility of their aircraft at night. This F6F-5N served with the Night Fighter Unit attached to VF-6 aboard *Hancock* (*NARA 80G-334227*)

dangerous dawn and dusk periods as they targeted both the night reconnaissance aircraft and dedicated bombers.

The first Night Fighter Unit pilot to become an ace was Lt(jg) Robert Humphrey assigned to VF-17, embarked in *Hornet*. Humphrey's first victory came during a pre-dawn heckler mission over the Kyushu airfields just before the main strike. He found a Navy Type 0 Transport ('Topsy') near Kanoya East airfield and shot it down, dropping his landing gear to stay with the slower transport aircraft.

Humphrey got a third share of a 'Myrt' on a late afternoon patrol on 23 March, and then shot down two aeroplanes during the course of a pre-dawn CAP on 27 March. Shortly before 0400 hrs Humphrey received a vector that led him to a large Navy Type 2 Flying Boat ('Emily'). Pulling up unobserved, he fired a burst into the right wing from 300 ft. The 'Emily' returned fire and started an evasive turn. Humphrey fired again into the right wing and watched as the flying boat spiralled down into the sea. A second vector shortly before dawn led him to a 'Jill' carrying a torpedo, which he shot down with three bursts.

Humphrey's next kill was a 'Betty' bomber, which he shot down on 17 April during a night CAP. Using his APS-6 radar, Humphrey closed on the 'Betty' and fired as it attempted evasive action, setting the starboard engine on fire. His second attack flamed the port engine. A third burst finished the 'Betty' off, the bomber rolling over and crashing into the water. His last victory was on 24 May when he shot down a Navy Zuiun Reconnaissance Seaplane ('Paul').

Two pilots in VF-83's Night Fighter Unit, Lt Donald Umphres and Ens James Barnes, also became aces. Barnes shot down a 'Sonia' before dawn on 4 April for his first victory. Two days later, during the first Kikusui operation, Lt Umphres destroyed a 'Betty' on a dawn CAP, and then led Barnes and Ens Somers on a dusk CAP over Okinawa. Given a vector, the division picked out three 'Vals' flying in loose formation despite the poor visibility. Umphres shot down the 'tail-end Charlie', while Barnes destroyed the second with a stern attack. With the third 'Val' headed directly for a radar picket destroyer, Barnes overtook the dive-bomber and fired several bursts into its wing. The 'Val' exploded and crashed into the sea just short of the destroyer.

The Night Fighter Unit assigned to VF-83 on *Essex* during the Okinawa campaign. Lt Donald Umphres is standing third from the left, while Ens James Barnes stands on the far right. Both naval aviators became aces during the Okinawa campaign (*via the author*)

Receiving a second vector, the three pilots found three 'Oscars' flying in a loose line-abreast formation. Umprhes made a run on the middle 'Oscar' and set it on fire, the pilot bailing out. He then attacked a second 'Oscar', which disintegrated under his fire. The third 'Oscar', clearly flown by an experienced pilot, turned and made head-on runs against both Umphres and Somers. Barnes eventually managed to get in a 60-degree deflection shot from behind the fighter, setting it on fire. The pilot

made 'a safe jump into a very empty ocean'. A third vector brought another aggressive 'Oscar', which again attacked Umphres and Somers with head-on runs until Barnes managed to get on the fighter's tail and shoot it down. He received the Navy Cross for his actions.

During a night CAP on 13 May, Umphres and Barnes both shot down 'Jake' floatplanes, Umphres later adding a 'Tony' that he spotted flying above the overcast. The 'Jake' had proven to be no easy victory for Umphres. Having initially made contact with a bogey that he misidentified as a 'Zeke' at 0245 hrs, he opened fire at close range but overshot the 'Jake' when its gunner opened fire on him. The floatplane then dove into the clouds below, but Umphres managed to find him using his radar, despite the 'Jake' jinking violently. Umphres lost contact with his target several times, but received vectors from the fighter director. After 30 minutes he finally managed to get a visual on the 'Jake'. Pulling in behind it, he fired a long burst and saw the floatplane explode.

Ens John Orth of VF-9's Night Fighter Unit had the distinction of getting multiple night kills on two occasions. He scored his first victory, an 'Irving', before dawn on 5 April. At month-end Orth took off on a night CAP over the task force just before midnight on 29 April. After an hour on station he was given a vector, and using his radar scope he picked up a contact that turned out to be four aircraft flying in loose formation. Getting a visual, Orth identified the lead machine as an 'Irving' with red and green wing lights and a white tail light showing. This may actually have been a 'Frances', the Fifth Air Fleet having sent out eight examples, and nine 'Betty' bombers, on a night attack against enemy shipping. Orth saw a 'Betty' to the left of the lead aircraft and two more on the right.

Closing in on the leader from behind and below, Orth fired three short bursts, setting the port engine on fire. The aeroplane rolled over and crashed into the sea. Orth then quickly slid to the left behind one of the 'Betty' bombers and fired several bursts to its wing and fuselage, which set the aircraft on fire. The 'Betty' went down into the water and exploded violently, the light temporarily blinding Orth so that he lost the two remaining aeroplanes.

Four days later on 4 May, Orth took off at 0300 hrs on a dawn CAP. Heading northwest of the task force, he was given a vector by the fighter director aboard USS *Randolph* (CV-15). Closing in on the bogey using

An F6F-5N from VF-9 blows a tyre landing back aboard *Yorktown*. In some squadrons the nightfighter Hellcats were designated with the letter N next to the aircraft number, as seen on the engine cowling of this machine (*NARA 80G-312546*)

Lt John Orth, who flew with the Night Fighter Unit attached to VF-9, received the Navy Cross for shooting down three 'Betty' bombers during a single nocturnal mission (*via the author*)

As the campaign progressed, land-based Marine Corps nightfighter squadrons took over responsibility for night patrols over Okinawa. This F6F-5N served with VMF(N)-533, the highest scoring Marine Corps nightfighter squadron of the campaign (*John Lambert Collection, Museum of Flight*)

Maj Gen Louis Woods, Tactical Air Force commander, congratulates Capt Robert Baird of VMF(N)-533, the Marine Corps' sole nightfighter ace of the Okinawa campaign (*NARA 127GW-128785*)

his radar scope, Orth dropped his wheels and flaps to match the speed of the enemy aircraft that he identified as a 'Betty' flying 300 ft above him and about a quarter-mile ahead. Orth initially flew alongside the 'Betty', before dropping back astern, opening fire and getting hits on the wings and fuselage. He continued firing as the 'Betty' turned to the left and right to avoid him, Orth again dropping his wheels and flaps to stay with the now burning bomber. By now well ablaze, the 'Betty', eventually hit the water and exploded.

Orth was then given another vector, which turned out to be yet another 'Betty'. Closing to 200-300 ft, Orth fired several bursts and sent the burning 'Betty' straight down into the sea.

Climbing back up to 8000 ft, he received a third vector and followed this to his third 'Betty' of the night, getting hits on the wings and engines, which again quickly set the 'Betty' on fire and sent it down to explode in the water. For this rare feat of shooting down three aircraft at night on a single mission, Orth received the Navy Cross.

Marine Corps land-based nightfighter squadrons claimed 68 enemy aircraft shot down, VMF(N)-533 being the high-scoring unit with 35 claims. Capt Robert Baird claimed six victories flying with VMF(N)-533 (see *Osprey Aircraft of the Aces 84 -American Nightfighter Aces of World War 2* for a full description of Baird's combats). He shot down five aircraft between 9 and 22 June, when the Okinawa campaign ended, and scored his sixth and final victory on 14 July.

NEAR ACES

The composite squadrons on the escort carriers of TG 52.1 (the Support Carrier Group) flew from the beginning to the end of the Okinawa campaign. While their primary mission was close air support and strikes on Japanese installations on Okinawa and the islands in the surrounding area, during the course of these missions, and on CAPs, the fighter pilots in the composite units shot down 280 Japanese aircraft.

With a more powerful engine, the General Motors-built FM-2 Wildcat fighters assigned to the composite squadrons were faster and had a much better climbing speed than the older Grumman-built F4F-4 versions of the Wildcat. They were more than adequate to take on the more venerable Japanese types such as the 'Val', 'Zeke', 'Oscar', 'Sonia', 'Nate' and twin-engined types that made up the bulk of equipment employed by the kamikaze Special Attack units. While their opportunities to engage in air combat were fewer than those of the fighter pilots on the Fast Carriers or the Marine Corps Corsair pilots on Okinawa, when the composite squadron fighter pilots did run into formations of Japanese aircraft they also managed to score multiple kills on a single mission. Lacking repeat opportunities meant that none of the composite units produced an ace, but several fighter pilots came tantalisingly close.

Lt(jg) Thomas Sedaker was the composite squadron fighter pilot who achieved the highest tally, being credited with a cumulative score of 4.833 kills flying with VC-84 off USS *Makin Island* (CVE-93). On 5 January 1945, off the coast of Luzon, Sedaker claimed a 'Zeke' and received a quarter share in two more, getting a one-third share in a 'Lily' bomber shot down the next day. He claimed a 'Val' on 27 March and two more dive-bombers on 12 April during the second Kikusui operation.

Lt David Sims, flying with VC-88 off USS *Saginaw Bay* (CVE-82), claimed four aircraft shot down and one damaged in two of the early April battles. Late in the afternoon of 2 April, while leading a division of four FM-2s, Sims was vectored onto several bogies closing in on the transports around Kerema Retto. Flying 2000 ft above a layer of cloud, Sims saw a 'Frances' flying slightly below him in a glide attack. Sims made a high side run and got hits in the wing roots, which caused the 'Frances' to start smoking but did not stop its glide. The ships began throwing up intense AAA, forcing Sims out of the area.

Climbing away, Sims found a second 'Frances', opening fire from the 'one o'clock' position and swinging around to the 'five o'clock' position as it flew past him. Sims got in good hits and the aircraft started smoking badly. It headed for the water from an altitude of less than 800 ft, although Sims did not see it crash. He then spotted a third 'Frances' flying just above the water heading for the transport ships. Coming in high from the 'three o'clock' position, Sims swung around behind the 'Frances' and set the aeroplane on fire. Its left wing hit the water and the bomber cartwheeled into the sea.

Five days later Sims was escorting a TBM Avenger on a photo-reconnaissance mission over Okinawa when both aircraft found themselves in the middle of a kamikaze raid on naval vessels offshore. Sims descended to investigate an aeroplane below him, which proved to be another TBM, and as he was climbing back up he saw several 'Vals' diving on US Navy minesweepers.

Lt Thomas Sedaker of VC-84 received this cake for completing the 2000th catapult launch from the escort carrier *Makin Island*. He was also the FM-2 Wildcat pilot who came closest to making ace during anti-kamikaze operations. Sedaker was credited with 4.833 victories over the Philippines and Okinawa (*NHHC NH 69831*)

An HVAR-equipped FM-2 Wildcat from VC-84 is launched from *Makin Island* on a pre-invasion strike on Okinawa at the end of March 1945. Pilots found that even with the drop tanks still attached to the wings of their fighters, the more powerful FM-2 was more than able to out-manoeuvre the older types of Japanese aircraft committed to kamikaze missions (*NARA 80G-313753*)

Sims started firing at the second 'Val' in the formation from maximum range while still in his climb, continuing to fire until it shot past him, went out of control and crashed into the water. Not to be outdone, the pilot of the TBM Sims was escorting made a head-on attack on the third 'Val', then pulled up so that his rear gunner could get off a burst too. As the 'Val' dived away Sims came up behind it and began firing. He followed the dive-bomber down until the aircraft burst into flames, exploded and crashed into the sea.

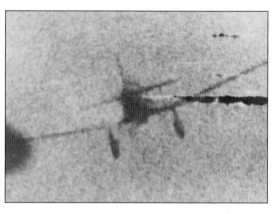

This photograph, taken from the VC-84 Aircraft Action Report of 7 April 1945, shows one of two 'Vals' shot down by Lt(jg) David Sims that day (*NARA*)

Lt Hatherly Foster III was the third composite squadron near-ace to come out of the Okinawa campaign. He was one of six Avenger pilots serving with VC-93 aboard USS *Petrof Bay* (CVE-80) who had hurriedly qualified in the FM-2 when the squadron's complement was increased from 12 to 18 fighters. Foster claimed his first victory on 6 April during the first Kikusui operation. Flying near Ie Shima, Foster's division ran into a 'Val' that had appeared out of cloud cover at 'nine o'clock'. The other aeroplanes in the division made a run on the 'Val', seemingly without success. Coming in last, Foster got on the tail of the aircraft, closed to 250 ft and opened fire. The 'Val' pilot chopped his throttle and dropped his flaps, forcing Foster to overrun, but the FM-2 pilot managed to get on the aircraft's tail again as it began a run on a destroyer escort below. Flying right into the AAA fire, Foster closed to 250 ft and fired into the 'Val's' right wing root, which exploded, sending the dive-bomber crashing into the sea just ahead of the destroyer.

Six days later Foster was again flying as the fourth man in a division on a CAP north of Okinawa during the second Kikusui operation. The division had already shot down several 'Vals' when they came across a single example flying on its own at 3000 ft. For the second time, Foster came in on the tail of the 'Val' after the other members of his division had fired on it without effect, setting the dive-bomber on fire. Shortly thereafter Foster saw an 'Oscar' beginning a dive onto a destroyer from 3500 ft. Ignoring the AAA fire coming up, Foster closed in on the 'Oscar's' tail and opened fire from 450 ft, closing to 100 ft. With smoke pouring out of its fuselage and wings, the 'Oscar' steepened its dive and crashed into the sea just 250 ft from the destroyer.

Five minutes later Foster saw a 'Zeke', which a Corsair had just missed shooting down, commence its glide attack on another destroyer. Foster went after the 'Zeke', pushing his FM-2's throttle into full military power. Getting on the fighter's tail, he opened fire at 500 ft and closed to within 150 ft, hitting the 'Zeke's' wings and engine. The aircraft began burning and hit the sea 400 ft from the destroyer. The AAA was so intense that several bursts could be seen on Foster's gun camera film. He had not had time to jettison his underwing drop tanks during the combat, yet despite this added drag his FM-2 had still out-performed all the Japanese aeroplanes he had encountered during the mission.

What had begun in the Philippines did not end until the Japanese surrender on 15 August 1945, although after the fall of Okinawa the JAAF and IJN launched only sporadic kamikaze attacks against American forces. Both services began hoarding Special Attack aeroplanes and pilots for the

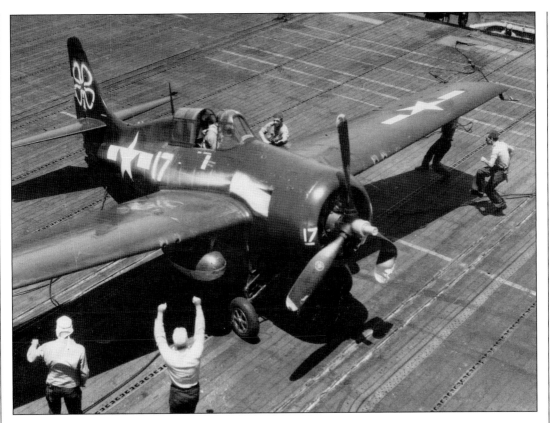

Ens Robert Myers flew this FM-2 Wildcat with VC-93 off *Petrof Bay*. He shot down two 'Zekes' and a 'Val' on 6 April 1945. Multiple kills were a common occurrence when encountering formations of poorly trained kamikaze pilots (*NARA 80G-378674*)

expected invasion of Japan. The Okinawa campaign had been the main battleground for the kamikaze. During the course of the ten Kikusui operations the IJN sent out approximately 860 Special Attack aircraft and the JAAF 605. Another 185 Special Attack sorties (140 from the IJN and 45 from the JAAF) were flown in between the Kikusui operations. An additional 250 Special Attack sorties were flown from bases on Formosa to targets in the Okinawa area, for a total of 1900 kamikaze sorties. The IJN and the JAAF lost an estimated additional 1100 conventional aircraft in combat during the Okinawa campaign.

From 18 March to 22 June US Navy fighter pilots claimed 1594 Japanese aircraft destroyed, Marine Corps pilots claimed 631 and USAAF pilots 101. During the course of the aerial battles over Okinawa and Kyushu 69 US Navy, 22 Marine Corps and five USAAF pilots were officially credited with five or more victories.

Casualties inflicted on the US Navy during the kamikaze campaigns in the Philippines and Okinawa were high. The US Strategic Bombing Survey, in its report on Japanese air power, deemed the 'single most effective air weapon developed by the Japanese to be the suicide aeroplane'. From the preliminary strikes on Kyushu on 18 March 1945 to the end of the campaign on 22 June 1945, kamikaze aircraft hit 216 warships, transports and auxiliaries – 26 of these vessels were sunk or had to be scuttled because of the severity of the damage. Nearly 5000 sailors were killed in the attacks. Painful as these losses were, they did not alter the outcome of the campaign. As in the Philippines, the kamikaze attacks were ultimately futile, with so many young lives sacrificed in vain.

APPENDICES

Aces of the Okinawa Campaign

Name	Unit	Okinawa Claims	Total Claims
Valencia, Lt Eugene	VF-9	12.5	23
French, Lt James	VF-9	10	11
Reber, Ens James	VF-30	10	11
Beebe, Lt Cdr Marshall	VF-17	9	10.5
Mitchell, Lt(jg) Harris	VF-9	9	10
Foster, Ens Carl	VF-30	8.5	8.5
Coleman, Lt Thaddeus	VF-83	8	10
Johnston, Lt(jg) John	VBF-17	8	8
Kirkwood, Lt(jg) Philip	VF-10	8	12
Miller, Ens Johnnie	VF-30	8	8
Reidy, Lt Thomas	VBF-83	8	10
Hibbard, Lt Samuel	VF-47	7.333	7.333
Brown, 2Lt William	VMF-311	7	7
Caswell, 2Lt Dean	VMF-221	7	7
Clark, Ens Lawrence	VF-83	7	7
Eckard, Lt Bert	VF-9	7	7
Harris, Lt(jg) Thomas	VF-17	7	7
Heath, Ens Horace	VF-10	7	7
Lerch, Ens Alfred	VF-30	7	7
O'Keefe, 1Lt Jeremiah	VMF-323	7	7
Ruhsam, 1Lt John	VMF-323	7	7
Ward, 1Lt Robert	VMF-323	7	7
Wolfe, Capt Judge	333rd FS/318th FG	7	9
Hardy, Lt(jg) Willis	VF-17	6.5	6.5
Watts, Lt(jg) Charles	VF-17	6.5	8.75
Dillard, 1Lt Joseph	VMF-323	6.333	6.333
Durnford, 2Lt Dewey	VMF-323	6.333	6.333
Terrill, 1Lt Francis	VMF-323	6.083	6.083
Axtell, Maj George	VMF-323	6	6
Barnes, Ens James	VF-83	6	6
Batten, Lt(jg) Hugh	VF-83	6	7
Brocato, Lt(jg) Samuel	VF-83	6	7
Clark, Ens Robert	VBF-17	6	6
Coats, Lt Robert	VF-17	6	9.333
Cowger, Lt Robert	VF-17	6	6
Dahms, Ens Kenneth	VF-30	6	7
Dorroh, Maj Jefferson	VMF-323	6	6
Eberts, Lt(jg) Byron	VBF-17	6	6
Freeman, Lt Doris	VF-84	6	9
Hamilton, Lt(jg) Robert	VF-83	6	6
Jennings, Lt Robert	VF-82	6	9.5
Kingston, Ens William	VF-83	6	6
McManus, 1Lt John	VMF-221	6	6
Mollard, Lt(jg) Norman	VF-45	6	6
Orth, Ens John	VF-9	6	6
Pool, Lt(jg) Tilman	VF-17	6	6
Quiel, Ens Norwald	VF-10	6	6
Smith, Lt(jg) John	VF-84	6	10
Snider, Capt William	VMF-221	6	11.5
Sturdevant, Lt(jg) Harvey	VF-30	6	6
Umphres, Lt Donald	VF-83	6	6
Valentine, Capt Herbert	VMF-312	6	6
Winfield, Lt(jg) Murray	VF-17	6	6
Yeremian, Ens Harold	VBF-17	6	6
Cain, Lt James	VF-45	5.5	8
Hood, 1Lt William	VMF-323	5.5	5.5
Kirkpatrick, Capt Floyd	VMF-441	5.5	5.5
Humphrey, Lt(jg) Robert	VF-17	5.333	5.333
Alley, 2Lt Stuart	VMF-323	5	5
Anderson, 1Lt Richard	19th FS/318th FG	5	5
Baird, Capt Robert	VMF(N)-533	5	6
Bolduc, Lt Alfred	VBF-12	5	5
Conant, Lt Edwin	VBF-17	5	7
Crosby, Lt(jg) John	VF-17	5	5.25
Davies, Lt(jg) Clarence	VF-82	5	5
Donahue, Maj Archie	VMF-451	5	14
Drake, 2Lt Charles	VMF-323	5	5
Farrell, 1Lt William	VMF-312	5	5
Gildea, Lt(jg) John	VF-84	5	5
Godson, Lt Lindley	VBF-83	5	5
Hoag, Ens John	VF-82	5	5
Johannsen, Ens Delmar	VBF-12	5	5
Kaelin, Ens Joseph	VF-9	5	5
Kincaid, Lt Robert	VBF-83	5	5
Kostik, Ens William	VBF-17	5	5
Lustic, 1Lt Stanley	19th FS/318th FG	5	5
Manson, Lt Armond	VF-82	5	7
Mathis, 1Lt William	19th FS/318th FG	5	5
Mayberry, Lt(jg) Lewin	VF-84	5	5
Mazzocco, Ens Michele	VF-30	5	5
McClure, Lt Edgar	VBF-9	5	5
McGinty, 1Lt Selva	VMF-441	5	5
McPherson, Ens Donald	VF-83	5	5
Mitchell, Lt(jg) Henry	VBF-17	5	6
Olsen, Ens Austin	VF-30	5	5
Pearce, Lt James	VF-17	5	5.25
Philips, Ens David	VF-30	5	5
Sistrunk, Lt(jg) Frank	VF-17	5	5
Smith, Lt(jg) Clinton	VF-9	5	6
Stone, Lt(jg) Carl Van	VBF-17	5	5
Vogt, Capt John	19th FS/318th FG	5	5
Ward, Ens Lyttleton	VF-83	5	5
Wells, 1Lt Albert	VMF-323	5	5

A Note on Late War Carrier Fighter Markings

Unlike their USAAF counterparts, towards the end of the war US Navy carrier fighter pilots rarely had their own individual aircraft. With around 100 aeroplanes assigned to each of the large *Essex*-class fleet carriers (of which some 70 were Hellcats, Corsairs or a combination of the two), all being constantly spotted and re-spotted on the flightdeck, or being taken below to the hangar deck for maintenance, it was impractical for the carrier's Air Department to arrange for a pilot to fly one specific aeroplane. Pilots flew whatever aircraft was assigned to them.

Typically, a squadron would tell the Air Department how many aircraft were needed for a particular mission, based on the number of divisions taking part. The Air Department would then spot that number of serviceable fighters on the flightdeck, in rows of four, for each of the divisions required. Aircraft would be assigned to the pilots in a division and the aircraft's 'plane in squadron', or tactical, number written next to the pilot's name on the blackboard in the squadron's ready room so the he could easily find his assigned aeroplane on the flightdeck. Once a pilot was in the cockpit, however, the only aircraft numbers he cared about were those on the other fighters in his division. While pilots recorded the Bureau of Aeronautics serial numbers (BuNos) of the aircraft they flew in their logbooks, few bothered to record the aircraft's tactical number, and few documents linking aircraft tactical numbers and BuNos have survived. In addition, aircraft came and went off a carrier continuously.

A carrier's Air Department was responsible for basic maintenance and minor repairs. When more thorough maintenance was required, an aeroplane would be flown back to a rear area base, overhauled and then returned to a Carrier Aircraft Service Unit pool for re-assignment. If an aeroplane was too damaged in combat to be repaired, it was stripped of parts and simply pushed over the side of the carrier. The combination of all these factors ultimately meant that pilots often flew many different aircraft during their combat tours. For example, VF-17 ace Lt(jg) Willis Hardy flew 57 different Hellcats whilst completing 90 combat missions over Okinawa.

While BuNo numbers are usually known, it is thus often difficult at this late date to determine with precision the exact tactical number of an aeroplane that a particular ace flew on a particular mission. While some units (notably VF-83) would sometimes paint kill markings on an aircraft used by pilots to claim specific victories, in many cases there simply was not time for such embellishments. A survey of photographs from the period indicates that kill markings, personal markings and squadron insignia were the exception rather than the rule – some squadrons adopted the practice and others didn't.

At the end of a combat tour, for publicity purposes, many squadrons would often take an aeroplane and pose each of the unit's pilots in the cockpit, with the pilot's kills shown below, but this may have been in a fighter that the naval aviator never actually flew in combat. For this reason a number of the colour plates in this book feature aeroplanes that are representative of the fighters the aces flew, and not necessarily the exact machine flown on a particular mission.

1

FM-2 Wildcat (BuNo unknown)/white 35 flown by Lt Ralph Elliott Jr, VC-27, USS *Savo Island* (CVE-78), January 1945

Lt Ralph Elliott received his wings in October 1941 and served as an instructor pilot for the next two years before joining Composite Squadron (VC) 27. This unit was assigned to USS *Savo Island* (CVE-78) from September 1944 to February 1945, and during this time it fought in the Philippines supporting the invasions of Luzon and Mindoro. Elliott shot down four 'Frances' bombers on his first encounter with Japanese aeroplanes on 24 October 1944 and claimed his last victories on 5 January 1945, thus becoming the top-scoring US Navy FM-2 pilot of the war with 9.5 victories to his name. Like other US Navy carrier fighter pilots, Elliot flew a number of Wildcats during his combat tour. Towards the end of the Philippine campaign Elliott was often at the controls of this FM-2, which carried his nine victories under the cockpit and was named *BALDY* after his brother's German Shepherd dog.

2

F6F-5 Hellcat (BuNo unknown)/white 17, VF-7, USS *Hancock* (CV-19), November 1944

At the start of the war Lt Cdr Leonard Check was a dive-bomber pilot with VB-6 aboard *Enterprise*. He became commanding officer of VF-7 when the squadron was commissioned in January 1944, and remained its CO until his death in a mid-air collision over Heito, Formosa, on 4 January 1945. During the Philippine campaign Check was given credit for ten Japanese aeroplanes shot down. By this time VF-7 was flying F6F-5 Hellcats in overall Glossy Sea Blue. With the introduction of many more 'flattops' into the fleet, carrier air groups had started using small geometric markings on the tail as a means of identification – Carrier Air Group 7 used a horseshoe symbol.

3

F6F-5 Hellcat (BuNo unknown)/white 47 flown by Lt Patrick Fleming, VF-80, USS *Ticonderoga* (CV-14), November 1944

A graduate of the US Naval Academy, Patrick Fleming spent a year as a flying instructor before being assigned to VF-80. He shot down ten aircraft during the Philippines campaign flying off *Ticonderoga*. As XO of VBF-80, flying off *Hancock*, Fleming claimed an additional nine aircraft during the February 1945 raids on Tokyo. He had the distinction of shooting down four Japanese fighters during a single mission on three occasions. 'White 47' is believed to be one of the Hellcats he flew with VF-80.

4

P-38L-5 Lightning 44-25327/black 19 flown by Lt Fernley Damstrom, 7th FS/49th FG, Tacloban, Leyte, December 1944

Lt Fernley Damstrom was the 7th FS's leading ace of the Philippines campaign with eight victories. All of his kills were obtained in the fighting over the Philippines. Damstrom was killed in a flying accident on 11 April 1945.

5

F6F-5 Hellcat (BuNo unknown)/white 3 flown by Lt Eugene Valencia, VF-9, USS *Yorktown* (CV-10), April 1945
Like other Hellcat pilots, Lt Eugene Valencia flew a number of different aircraft during his second combat tour in 1945. In January 1945 the US Navy introduced a system of 28 larger and more visible geometric markings, called 'G' markings, for carrier-based aircraft to be painted in white on the tail, the uppersurface of the starboard wing and the undersurface of the port wing. On the larger fleet carriers the symbol designated the vessel, not the carrier air group. VF-9 shifted from *Lexington* to *Yorktown* in March 1945, adopting the latter's white tail symbol.

6

F6F-5N Hellcat (BuNo unknown)/white 4 flown by Ens John Orth, VF-9, USS *Yorktown* (CV-10), May 1945
Flying as 'Nan 4', Ens John Orth is believed to have used this aircraft on the 4 May 1945 mission that saw him shoot down three 'Betty' bombers – a feat that earned him the Navy Cross. A number of the Night Fighter Units assigned to the *Essex*-class carriers appear to have painted out the white geometric 'G' markings on their aircraft to reduce their visibility at night, leaving only the white national insignia. Nightfighters also appear to have carried single-digit 'plane in squadron' numbers, usually from 1 to 6, prefixed with the letter N.

7

F4U-1D Corsair (BuNo unknown)/white 66 flown by Ens Alfred Lerch, VF-10, USS *Intrepid* (CV-11), April 1945
On 16 April 1945, VF-10 claimed 32 aircraft shot down during a series of early morning battles. Ens Alfred Lerch claimed six 'Nates' and a 'Val', Lt(jg) Philip Kirkwood downed six aircraft and two other pilots from the unit claimed four apiece.

8

F6F-5 Hellcat (BuNo unknown)/white 66 of VF/VBF-12, USS *Randolph* (CV-15), April-May 1945
In January 1945 the US Navy divided the recently enlarged fighter squadrons on the larger *Essex*-class carriers into separate fighter (VF) and fighter-bomber (VBF) units for ease of administration. In carrier air groups where the VF and VBF squadrons flew the same aircraft type, such as VF/VBF-9, VF/VBF-12 and VF/VBF-17, the 72 embarked fighters were used interchangeably between the two units. White 66 had *Randolph*'s 'G' markings on the tail and a non-standard and crudely applied 'plane in squadron' number below the cockpit.

9

F6F-5 Hellcat (BuNo unknown)/white 35 flown by Lt James Pearce, VF-17, USS *Hornet* (CV-12), 18-21 March 1945
Before the attacks on the Kyushu airfields and the IJN fleet at Kure, TF 58's fighters had a white band painted around the cowl as an easily recognisable identification marking. This was in addition to the Fleet 'G' markings – in this case

two white squares on the tail for *Hornet*. White 35 was one of several VF-17 aircraft that had a small 'Jolly Roger' emblem (the squadron insignia) painted ahead of the cockpit. During the March raids Lt James Pearce flew five different Hellcats.

10

F6F-5 Hellcat BuNo 72748/white 33 flown by Lt(jg) Willis Hardy, VF-17, USS *Hornet* (CV-12), 6 April 1945
Lt(jg) Willis Hardy made his fifth kill of 6 April just as the sun was setting. Following a vector, he and his wingman came up on a 'Judy'. By now only one gun in Hardy's Hellcat was still operable, and his wingman's weapons were out of ammunition. While the latter made feint attacks on the 'Judy', forcing it to turn toward him, Hardy got off three or four bursts at a time, then had to re-charge his gun. Dropping his flaps and turning inside the 'Judy', Hardy managed to aim several bursts into the cockpit, setting the 'Judy' on fire.

11

F6F-5 Hellcat (BuNo unknown)/white 10 of VF-30, USS *Belleau Wood* (CVL-24), April 1945
Flying Hellcats in these markings, Ens Kenneth Dahms, Carl Foster and Johnnie Miller all became 'aces in a day' during VF-30's best day of the war – 6 April 1945. At the end of the unit's combat tour Ens James Reber, VF-30's leading ace with 11 victories, and Ens Carl Foster with 8.5 victories were photographed in Hellcats marked up with their final tallies. These shots were run in US newspapers.

12

F6F-5 Hellcat BuNo 72522/blue 7 flown by Lt James Cain, VF-45, USS *San Jacinto* (CVL-30), 23 March 1945
Blue 7 was one of 25 Hellcats that Lt James Cain flew off *San Jacinto* during the Okinawa campaign. He was at the controls of this particular F6F on 23 March 1945, when VF-45 conducted pre-invasion strikes on the islands around Okinawa. Cain's best day was also on 6 April 1945, when he claimed 3.5 victories flying Hellcat BuNo 71912.

13

F6F-5 Hellcat (BuNo unknown)/blue 16, VF-47, USS *Bataan* (CVL-29), April-May 1945
Lt Samuel 'Mother' Hibbard was VF-47's only ace, claiming 7.333 victories. Before joining VF-47, he had flown PBM Mariner patrol flying boats with VPB-214. Hibbard's best day was on 16 April 1945, when he accounted for two 'Zekes' – VF-47 pilots claimed 23 aircraft that day.

14

F6F-5 Hellcat (BuNo unknown)/white 74, VF-82, USS *Bennington* (CV-20), April-May 1945
VF-82 produced four aces during the Okinawa campaign, and Lt Robert Jennings was the squadron's leading scorer with six victories during the campaign. This boosted his wartime total to 9.5. Jennings had flown F4F Wildcats with VF-72 in 1942-43, claiming 2.5 victories, and he added another during the February 1945 strikes on Tokyo. He received the Navy Cross following the 19 March mission to Kure, having braved intense AAA to hit an IJN aircraft carrier in the harbour with his bombs and rockets .

15

F6F-5 Hellcat (BuNo unknown)/white 111 possibly flown by Lt Thaddeus Coleman, VF-83, USS *Essex* (CV-9), April-May 1945

VF-83 was the second-highest scoring US Navy fighter squadron during the Okinawa campaign with 134 claims between 18 March and 22 June 1945 – 11 of its pilots became aces. The squadron had a practice of recording an aircraft's victories below the cockpit, white 111 being marked with eight victories that could possibly have represented the score of Lt Thaddeus Coleman, who claimed eight kills between 31 March and 14 May. This aeroplane was used as a backdrop for photographs of each of VF-83's divisions in the Carrier Air Group 83 cruise book published in 1946.

16

F6F-5 Hellcat (BuNo unknown)/white 126 of VF-83, USS *Essex* (CV-9), April-May 1945

White 126 was another of VF-83's Hellcats with kill markings displayed beneath the cockpit, in this case representing claims for nine Japanese aircraft. White 126 was almost certainly flown by a number of pilots who made claims in it.

17

F4U-1D Corsair (BuNo unknown)/white 185 of VBF-83, USS *Essex* (CV-9), April-May 1945

VBF-83, sister-squadron to VF-83, appears to have followed a similar practice in painting kill markings on its Corsairs, white 185 having six such symbols beneath its cockpit. At least one other Corsair – white 174 – also had six kill markings painted on. VBF-83 claimed 86 Japanese aircraft and produced three aces during the Okinawa campaign.

18

F4U-1D Corsair (BuNo unknown)/white 133 flown by Lt Doris 'Chico' Freeman, VF-84, USS *Bunker Hill* (CV-17), April-May 1945

Carrier Air Group 84 had one US Navy (VF-84) and two Marine Corps Corsair squadrons (VMF-221 and VMF-451) assigned to it, with a complement of around 60 aircraft – mostly F4U-1Ds, with a small number of F4U-1C Corsairs (the three units used these fighters interchangeably). On 17 April 1945, Lt Doris 'Chico' Freeman downed a 'George' flying F4U-1D white 133 for his second of six kills during the Okinawa campaign.

19

FM-2 Wildcat (BuNo unknown)/white 18, VC-88, USS *Saginaw Bay* (CVE-82), April 1945

The escort carriers of TG 52.1 had their own system of geometric markings, *Saginaw Bay* using two lightning bolts on the tail. Lt(jg) David Sims was flying an FM-2 in these markings when he shot down two 'Vals' on 7 April 1945. He narrowly missed becoming an ace, claiming four Japanese aircraft shot down and a fifth damaged during early April.

20

FM-2 Wildcat (BuNo unknown)/white 17 flown by Ens Robert Myers, VC-93, USS *Petrof Bay* (CVE-80), April 1945

Petrof Bay used a large four-leafed clover as the identifying marking for its assigned squadron, VC-93. This unit claimed 17 Japanese aircraft shot down during the Okinawa campaign, Lt(jg) Hatherly Foster III being the squadron's most successful pilot with four victories. Ens Robert Myers had three kills (two 'Zekes' and a 'Val'), all of which were claimed during the Kikusui Operation No 1 on 6 April 1945.

21

FM-2 Wildcat (BuNo unknown)/white 11, VC-84, USS *Makin Island* (CVE-93), April 1945

Makin Island used a simple white bar on the tail to identify the FM-2 Wildcats and TBM Avengers assigned to VC-84. White 11 is representative of the Wildcats Lt(jg) Thomas Sedaker flew on close air support sorties and CAPs during the month of April.

22

F4U-1D Corsair (BuNo unknown)/white 183 flown by 2Lt Dean Caswell, VMF-221, USS *Bunker Hill* (CV-17), 28 April 1945

Caswell is believed to have been flying this aircraft during his most difficult combat mission when he and the two other members of his division ran into a large formation of Zero-sen fighters. Caswell received credit for downing three 'Zekes', with a fourth fighter claimed as a probable. This was the second mission during which Caswell shot down three enemy aircraft.

23

F4U-1C Corsair (BuNo unknown)/white 310 of VMF-311, Yontan airfield, Okinawa, June 1945

VMF-311 was equipped with the cannon-armed F4U-1C version of the Corsair, and it arrived at Okinawa's Yontan airfield on 7 April 1945. White 310 had a remarkable record with the squadron, surviving months of combat on Okinawa. By the end of the campaign this aeroplane had accumulated more than 400 combat hours, shot down eight of the 71 aircraft credited to VMF-331 and flown numerous ground support and strike missions over Okinawa and the Japanese mainland.

24

F4U-1D Corsair (BuNo unknown)/white 530 of VMF-312, Yontan airfield, Okinawa, April-May 1945

VMF-312 painted its Corsairs with white chequerboard markings on the nose and tail as a recognition feature. The unit produced two aces during the Okinawa campaign, namely 1Lt William Farrell and Capt Herbert Valentine. Farrell claimed 4.5 flying BuNo 76303 on 25 May, while Valentine claimed 5.5 kills in BuNo 57670 that same day.

25

F4U-1D Corsair (BuNo unknown)/white 26 flown by 1Lt Jeremiah O'Keefe, VMF-323, Yontan airfield, Okinawa, April 1945

O'Keefe scored all seven of his aerial victories over two days – 22 and 28 April 1945. On the 22nd he became an 'ace in a day' during his very first experience of aerial combat. Squadronmates Majs George Axtell and Jefferson Dorroh also made 'ace in a day' on 22 April. All three were awarded the Navy Cross. O'Keefe was two months short of his 22nd birthday when he became an ace, having been a Marine Corps pilot for a little under two years.

26

F4U-1D Corsair (BuNo unknown)/white 5 of VMF-323, Yontan airfield, Okinawa, May-June 1945

VMF-323 also marked up individual aircraft with the total number of kills the aircraft had achieved whilst being flown by different pilots. White 5 had ten kill markings, representing the victories of a number of pilots. VMF-323 was the highest scoring Marine fighter squadron of the Okinawa campaign with 124.5 victories.

27

F4U-1D Corsair (BuNo unknown)/white 422 *Palpitatin' Pauli* flown by Capt Floyd Kirkpatrick, VMF-441, Yontan airfield, Okinawa, 28 April 1945

Capt Floyd Kirkpatrick named his aeroplane after his wife. Photographs of him taken with this fighter show 3.5 kills, representing three 'Vals' claimed on 16 April and a half-share in a 'Zeke' 12 days later. Kirkpatrick was one of two pilots who made ace with VMF-441, the other being 1Lt Selva McGinty. VMF-441 claimed 47 Japanese aircraft destroyed during the Okinawa campaign.

28

F4U-1D Corsair (BuNo unknown)/white 141 flown by Maj Archie Donahue, VMF-451, USS *Bunker Hill* (CV-17), 12 April 1945

Maj Archie Donahue served as the XO of VMF-451, which was one of four Marine Corps Corsair squadrons that served aboard *Essex*-class carriers during the Okinawa campaign. Donahue was an experienced fighter pilot, having joined the Marine Corps before America's entry into the war. He was also one of a number of US Navy and Marine Corps aces who added to their scores during the Okinawa campaign.

29

F6F-5N Hellcat (BuNo unknown)/black F(N)4 flown by Capt Robert Baird, VMF(N)-533, Yontan airfield, Okinawa, June 1945

VMF(N)-533 was one of eight Marine Corps nightfighter units activated during the war, and it ultimately became the highest scoring nightfighter squadron during the Okinawa campaign

with 35 victories. VMF(N)-533 arrived on Okinawa on 10 May 1945, although Capt. Baird – the highest scoring Marine Corps nightfighter pilot of World War 2 – did not get the first of his six victories until 9 June.

30

P-47N Thunderbolt, 44-87962/black 10 *BOTTOM'S UP* flown by 1Lt William Mathis, 19th FS/318th FG, Ie Shima, May-June 1945

1Lt Mathis was one of a number of pilots who participated in the Okinawa campaign and became aces during a limited number of encounters with Japanese aeroplanes – indeed, Mathis managed to score his five victories in only two combats. The individual aircraft number on Thunderbolt *BOTTOM'S UP* is not known for certin, but the 19th FS used numerals in the 01 to 37 range. The squadron painted its insignia on its P-47Ns.

31

P-47N Thunderbolt 44-87911/black 04 *DRINK'N SISTER* of Capt John Vogt, 19th FS/318th FG, Ie Shima, 28 May 1945

When Capt John Vogt entered combat in May 1945 he had more than 1300 hours of flying time and had been with the 318th FG for nearly 18 months. He put this experience to good use during his only encounter with Japanese aircraft, shooting down five 'Zekes' and claiming a sixth as a probable. For his actions on this mission Vogt was awarded the Distinguished Service Cross.

32

P-47N Thunderbolt 44-87959 flown by Capt Judge Wolfe, 333rd FS/318th FG, Ie Shima, May-June 1945

Capt Wolfe was another experienced fighter pilot who had more than 1000 hours of flying time to his name when he arrived on Okinawa in May 1945. Wolfe had previously claimed two 'Betty' bombers flying a P-38 in February 1945. With his victories during the Okinawa campaign, he became the 318th FG's leading ace. At this time the 333rd FS did not assign individual numbers to its aircraft, but like the 19th FS, its P-47Ns were adorned with the 333rd's squadron insignia.

BIBLIOGRAPHY

Caswell, Col Dean (USMC Ret), *Fighting Falcons - The Saga of Marine Fighter Squadron 221,* Privately Published

Condon, John Pomeroy, *Corsairs and Flatops - Marine Carrier Air Warfare, 1944-1945,* Naval Institute Press, 1998

Craven, W F and J L Cate, *The Army Air Forces in World War II Volume V - The Pacific-Matterhorn to Nagasaki (June 1944 to August 1945),* University of Chicago Press, 1953

Gandt, Robert:, *The Twilight Warriors,* Broadway Books, 2010

Hata, Ikuhio, Yasuho Izawa and Christopher Shores, *Japanese Naval Air Force Fighter Units and Their Aces 1932-1945,* Grub Street, 2011

Inoguchi, Rikihei, Tadashi Nakajima and Roger Pineau, *The Divine Wind - Japan's Kamikaze Force in World War II,* Naval Institute Press 1958

Japanese Monograph Series No 51 - *Air Operations on Iwo Jima and the Ryukus*

Japanese Monograph Series No 86 - *5th Air Fleet Operations February-August 1945*

Lambert, John W, *The Pineapple Air Force - Pearl Harbor to Tokyo,* Phalanx Publishing Co Ltd, 1990

Lamont-Brown, Raymond, *Kamikaze - Japan's Suicide Samurai,* Rigel Publications, 1997

Model Art Company Ltd, *Model Art No 451 - Rikugun Tokubetsu Kogeki-Tai (Imperial Japanese Army Air Force Suicide Attack Unit),* Model Art Company Ltd, 1995

Model Art Company Ltd, *Model Art No 458 - Kamikaze Tokubetsu Kogeki-Tai (Imperial Japanese Navy Air Force Suicide Attack Unit 'Kamikaze'),* Model Art Company Ltd, 1995

Morris, Ivan, *The Nobility of Failure - Tragic Heroes in the History of Japan,* Holt, Rinehart and Winston, 1975

Morrison, Samuel Elliot, *History of United States Naval Operations in World War II - Volume XII Leyte June 1944-January 1945; Volume XIII The Liberation of the Philippines: Luzon, Mindanao, the Visayas 1944-1945; Volume XIV The Victory in the Pacific 1945,* Little, Brown and Company, 1958-60

Pearce, Jim, *A 20th Century Guy,* Sonya Steiner Associates, 2007

Reilly, Robin L, *Kamikazes, Corsairs and Picket Ships - Okinawa 1945,* Casemate, 2008

Reilly, Robin L, *Kamikaze Attacks of World War II - A Complete History of Japanese Suicide Strikes on American Ships by Aircraft and Other Means,* McFarland & Company, 2010

Reynolds, Clark G, *The Fast Carriers - The Forging of an Air Navy,* McGraw Hill Book Company, 1968

Sherrod, Robert, *History of Marine Corps Aviation in World War II,* Association of the US Army, 1952

Wolf, William, *Death Rattlers - Marine Squadron VMF-323 Over Okinawa,* Schiffer Publishing Ltd, 1999

Youngblood, William T, *The Little Giants - US Escort Carriers Against Japan,* Naval Institute Press, 1987

INDEX